MW00561710

Instant Songwriting

Musical Improv from Dunce to Diva

by

Nancy Howland Walker

Satyagraha
Publishing

Published by Satyagraha Publishing, Kissimmee, FL USA

ISBN 978-0-9854652-4-7

Library of Congress Control Number: 2012911958

Edited by Katie O'Sullivan

The following songs are reprinted with permission:

"Over the Rainbow" (From "The Wizard of Oz")
Music by HAROLD ARLEN Lyrics by E.Y. HARBURG
Copyright © 1938 (Renewed) METRO-GOLDWYN-MAYER INC.
© 1939 (Renewed) EMI FEIST CATALOG INC.
All Rights Controlled and Administered by EMI FEIST CATALOG INC. (Publishing)
and ALFRED MUSIC PUBLISHING CO., INC. (Print)
All Rights Reserved Used by Permission

"The Ballad of the Shape of Things" by Sheldon Harnick
Copyright © 1950 by Sheldon Harnic
Copyright Renewed. International Copyright Secured. All Rights Reserved.
Used by Permission of Mayerling Productions LTD., administered by Williamson Music, A
Division of Rodgers & Hammerstein: An Imagem Company

"Peace" by Marshall Stern
Copyright 1994 by Marshall Stern
All Rights Reserved

Dedication

This book is dedicated to my wonderful husband Marshall "Sweetie" Stern. We wouldn't have met and become friends if not for musical improv. In the summer of 1999, Marshall had won a scholarship to study at Players Workshop of the Second City. A friend of his dragged him kicking and screaming to my weekend musical improv class. It should be understood that Marshall was a professional songwriter in Nashville at the time, and he HATED musical improv. But lo and behold, he LOVED the class - besides being fun and having a very intelligent and sexy teacher, it freed him up from over-thinking songs. His improv songs got immensely better, and he got unblocked for his written songs. We now teach musical improv together, among other improv classes (check out our Zenprov podcast on iTunes or at www.cia.libsyn.com!) We live each day with laughter on our lips and songs in our hearts!

Contents

Acknowledgements

When you are a first-time author (and writing on a budget!), you rely on wonderful, wonderful friends and co-workers and even strangers to help you through the process. First and foremost, I want to thank my Editor Katie Flohr O'Sullivan for spending so much time and expertise with me. Thanks also to Jerry Schulman, for legal help (hey - when you're quoting songs, you have to be careful!), Mike Brown for additional publishing legal advice, and cover artist Dick Hannus with Hannus Design and John Cremer who kept me from making any design faux pas. My thanks to Charna Halpern, who agreed to write the foreword without a moment's hesitation, even though she is the busiest woman in improv! Also huge thanks to all my contributing musicians. Their tracks make this book a practical course so readers can gain actual experience, rather than just theoretical knowledge. Special shout-out to Michael Pollock for going the extra mile and reading the entire book to give me a fabulous quote for my back cover. Thanks to all the wonderful cast members of *MUSICAL! the musical*, and all the improvisers I've sung with over the years. And finally a tip of the hat to Marshall Stern who helped me get my website and audio tracks working. Big love and thanks to you all!

Foreword

I am a lover of improvised musical theater and am constantly impressed when a performer can create a song on the spot that is as good - nay better - than songs that are written. I have an amazing musical troupe at iO, my Chicago theater and one in LA at iOWEST. So often a student will ask me how to get good enough to get on one of these performance troupes and I really don't have much of a way to help them - short of taking a series of our music classes. But even that can be scary. Then, I found a way to help. I read Nancy's book in the privacy of my own home. I found myself following the exercises and trying them - right there in my living room. I was having a blast. This book breaks it down and helps a student start from the very beginning. I will now recommend it to all my improv students as well as Musical Directors who can use her exercises in their classes. Nancy Howland Walker makes you want to sing.

- Charna Halpern, Artistic Director, iO

Introduction

I love to sing. I've always sung. I was the type of little kid who made up ditties (you could barely call them "songs") and sang them all over the place. Especially when I was out exploring the creek in the "Way Back" of our yard. Singing and nature just went together very happily.

Many years later, when I was a member of ImprovBoston, I was extremely happy when Steve Gilbane joined our group as our first accompanist. We started doing musical games and eventually a long-form musical. I was in heaven!

That love of musical improv led me to teach the art form, and eventually create a critically acclaimed show called *MUSICAL! the musical*, which was the country's first two-act completely improvised Broadway styled musical.

I've learned a lot from performing, teaching, producing and directing musical improv for nearly two decades. This book is the result.

This is a book for improvisers to add an important tool to their improv repertoire. It's a book for songwriters to get out of their heads and past their blocks. To learn, practice and gain the numerous skills involved in (instant) songwriting. I hope this book can help people reconnect with their joyous, singing child within.

It doesn't matter if you have a good singing voice. In most improv situations, a good voice is nice, but it's the commitment – the utter throwing yourself into the style and attitude of the song – that gets the rapt attention of the audience, and often has them rolling in the aisles.

And you know so much more than you think you do. Maybe you don't know all the technical theoretical terms, but our culture is very musically savvy. I mean, there's music playing everywhere – at home, in the car, at the mall, etc., etc. We hear it from a very young age. As a society, we are musically sophisticated. So you KNOW what sounds right or what just sounds off. Trust yourself.

Music is very powerful. I have an excellent friend, Randy Craig, whose brother had cancer. The prognosis was not good, but he refused treatment, convinced that God would save him if he had enough faith. And when Randy's brother asked God what to do, he was answered: "Sing." So he sang. Everywhere he went, he sang. And he sang. I know this sounds like an extremely hokey movie of the week, but it's absolutely true. When Randy's brother went back to the doctor, the cancer was in remission. It's 20 years later, and he's still cancer free. The Lesson? Singing makes you Alive!

Part 1

Musical Improv 101
(Dunce Level)

Chapter 1
Before You Start

Fun

The first thing I make all my students do is to stand up, lift one leg up in the air while raising both arms up high and say really loudly, "Wheee!"

Do it. Do it now. Or, if it would be just too embarrassing right now, do it at your earliest convenience.

Most of my students will do it. After all, it's in a safe, fun environment where others are doing it. But some refuse, thinking it makes them look silly or stupid. To them I say, "So what?!" Free yourself from the *concept* you have of yourself. Free yourself from the fear of what others think of you. Wheee!

But I digress. I don't make my students say "Wheee!' to teach them about their fears and blocks. I do it so they come to the experience with a good, fun attitude.

'Cause you gotta have fun. If you're not, then you're not learning as much as you can be. I've taught for many, many years, and I've seen that the students who have fun learn so much faster (and so much more) than those taking everything too seriously. They smile and laugh more often, thus making them happier and healthier.

So, by gum, have fun!

Warm Up Your Body

I also recommend stretching before you do creative things, like taking a class, doing an improv show, or writing.

Your body and mind are linked. If your body is tense, your mind will also be tense. Ideas won't flow as easily as they could. (Of course, relax your body naturally, Dude!)

Most of us hold tension in our necks and shoulders. The first thing I do is neck rolls – roll my head in a few circles each way – and shoulder rolls – forward and backwards a few times.

Do neck and shoulder rolls now, plus a couple of good, deep breaths.

If you can, stretch your spine and sides. The more muscles you stretch the better.

Warm Up Your Brain

You gotta warm up your brain synapses, too. And the brain to mouth connection. You can be thinking the most brilliant things in the world, but if you can't articulate them, it won't much matter.

Do a little word association with yourself. If you have another person who can do it with you, that's great. But you can do it by yourself. Just strive to get faster and faster.

Start by saying one word out loud. It doesn't matter what – anything. Then say the first associated word that comes to your mind. If you're doing this alone, anything you say will somehow be connected in your brain. If you're playing with more than one person, make sure you all are associating with the *last* word spoken – not just saying a list of pre-thought up words. Anyone can think of words ahead of time. The point is to make your thinking faster.

And no judging! Any and every word is okay. I do notice that sometimes when I'm not warmed up, my brain will think of 1,2, or even 3 words before my mouth has a chance to actually say a different word. I don't feel like I'm consciously editing myself, but at some level

I am. So the more I'm warmed up, the more I can say exactly what my brain thinks. It's all fine. Just notice how your brain works. It's always good to be aware of yourself!

Here – let me do an example right now: "ball, base, face, nose, spite, malice, vengeance, stab, pain, ass, donkey, Kong, King, Royal, tire…" That's how MY brain works. Hey! Spite and Malice is a card game my Grandmother used to play when I was little – I totally forgot about that game.

Do a quick word association for about a minute right now.

Fabulous.

Warm Up Your Voice

Let's warm up the voice, too, shall we? If you know you're going to be singing in class or on stage, please warm up your voice. Sure, you could do it without warming up. You also could go for a run without stretching first, but it's easier to get injured that way. Same thing for singing. Stretch your vocal chords first so you don't hurt yourself.

Track 1 has some vocal warm-ups for you now. You can use these warm-ups before a show, too. The first exercise goes up, the second goes down, and the third is an enunciation warm-up that goes, "Many mumbling mice, are making midnight music in the moonlight – migh-ty nice." (I believe that's from Dr. Seuss. Or Gilbert and Sullivan. Same thing!)

The musical track accompaniment can be found at this book's website: **www.InstantSongwriting.com**. You may listen to the tracks there or download them directly to your computer. You can also subscribe to the podcast with these tracks on iTunes.

When warming up, don't strain your voice – we go pretty high and low on these scales because someone with a very high or low voice might be singing along. If it starts feeling too strained, just drop an octave (or raise an octave if going down) and continue. Stretch your voice a bit – don't strain it.

Play TRACK 1 for vocal warm-ups.

Brilliant! You are now very superficially warmed up.

> ∿∿∿∿∿
>
> Please Note: For all the exercises, read all of the instructions first and THEN play the track and do the exercise. In the instructions, I say to play the track and do this, this, this, watch out for this, etc. Read it all and then play the track when it actually says "Play Track X" in italics.
>
> ∿∿∿∿∿

Emotion/Selling it!

As stated in the Introduction, you don't NEED a great voice to do musical improv. But it is essential to sell the song to the audience. That means you need to really sell the style and emotion of the song. Most audience members can't imagine singing in front of other people, much less making it up as they go along. So you're already ahead of the game. But when you really throw yourself into the song, they will LOVE it! (Many of these early exercises are more focused on the improviser/performer, but songwriters, it's good for you to know as well!)

So here's a great exercise for feeling the power of the music and translating it to song…

Exercise 1 – Hearing the Emotion of the Music/ Selling It!

Tracks 2 through 6 each has an emotional musical accompaniment. For each track/emotion, I want you to go through the following steps:

1. LISTEN to the music. Hear the style of the music. What kind of emotion does it evoke? Discover what kind of character would be singing to this music, in what kind of situation.

2. FEEL the emotion. Really try to exaggerate the emotion in your mind – it will help so much when you start adding words!

3. SHOW the emotion! I should be able to look at your face and know from your expression. Even more importantly, that emotion should flow through your entire body. Even if I can't see your face, I should be able to tell from your back if you're tense, or sad, or gleeful.

4. MOVE to the music in this emotion. A pissed-off person moves completely differently from a person in love. Have the music emotionally flow through your body. As you move, again discover what your character's situation is – did you just break up with your significant other? Did you just win the lottery? Did your roommates eat your jell-o pudding pops that you bought after you telling them your food was strictly off limits?!

This embodiment of the emotion is very important, and improvisers tend to forget about it – they're so busy being stuck in their heads coming up with ways to be witty/funny, or coming up with rhymes, that they have to work much harder than they have to, since they aren't connected to anything. Connecting your emotions, mind and body together like this will make it easier for getting out of your head and letting improv and songs flow naturally. (In Zen, it's called Wu Wei – Effortless Effort!) This emotional and physical connection is also huge in committing to the song and selling it when performing.

5. Start vocalizing your emotion. I ring a bell once in Track 2 and 3 to signal this step, and leave it up to you when to do it in the other tracks. (I purposely leave a lot of time for the "getting in touch and moving with your emotions" part in these two tracks, because improvisers tend to speed through these steps.) No words just yet. Sing on a "La la" or "Tee tee" or "Ooooooo" or "Aaaahhhhhhh" - whatever floats your boat as long as it goes with the emotion you're feeling.

Let me HEAR the emotion in your voice - in how you sing your "la la las." An angry "la la la" sounds very different from a joyous "la la la." If I could see you, I'd want to see the emotion expressed in your entire body (not *just* your face – where a LOT of actors put their emotion). Watch out for losing your emotion simply because you're vocalizing - feel the emotion and let it come out in your voice.

Make sure as you vocalize that your notes are going up and down and not just sitting on one level. As you get more upset, or joyful, or whatever, you may find your notes going generally up or getting louder (or a more intense softer – always a great choice!) It doesn't matter, as long as there is variety. People never speak all at one pitch and volume. You shouldn't either when you are singing!

6. When the bell rings twice in Tracks 2 and 3, and whenever you feel it in the other tracks, I want you to stop where you are (you should have been moving around!), plant yourself solidly, and put words to what you're feeling. Do not worry about rhyming or meter or anything like that. You are simply singing out loud what you are thinking and feeling as that character. The words may be about what just happened to your character, or what the character is planning to do. Perhaps the words describe images the character is seeing right now. (You imagine that you just lost your spouse and are sitting at the window looking out – perhaps you sing of the tattered curtains and rain falling on the lonely swing set outside…)

Remember to have variety – just because you started putting words in does not mean you have to go to one note and one level of emotion (like most improvisers do!) Again, watch out for losing your emotional intensity simply because you're singing words. Feel the emotion all through your body. The important words will tend to be high, or sustained, or loud, or repeated. (Or perhaps all four – i.e. "Scallywag! He is a scallywag! Why do I always have to fall for a SCAAALLYYYY-WAAAAAAAAAAG!!!![held long and high])

This is not to say that you never move when singing. Just don't lose your emotion, and move with purpose.

> ∩∪∩∪∩∪∩
>
> The ability to plant yourself solidly on the ground is important. You'll see most improvisers walk around randomly when they start singing, which can be distracting to the audience and really not helpful to the singer. When you stand/sit in one place it's possible to focus on your emotion more, you seem more confident, and look more legit, especially if you're doing the style of musical theater. Watch any Broadway musical and how the actors move and stand when they start singing. They don't randomly walk around. If they move, they move with purpose. And when they stand in one place, it's as if the well of emotion is so strong, that they CAN'T move – that it's GOT to be expelled from their psyche in song!
>
> ∪∩∪∩∪∩∪

7. END the section. You'll hear the music start to wrap up. Or you should – watch being sooooo involved in your emotion that you aren't aware of the music or other people that might be on stage. Of course, a good live musician will follow you wherever you go, but know that it should be a good give-and-take. When

you hear the music wrapping up, finish whatever you're singing
– you can hold out your last note to end when the music does
or before – and hold that emotion and physical pose until even
after the music stops.

∩∪∩∪∩∪∩

I've seen (way too often!) musical improvisers finish
their part of the song and drop their emotion and
character before the music ends! Please get in the
habit of staying in character and holding the intensity of what's happening until the lights go down,
you walk off stage, or the scene changes. You might
feel embarrassed for what you just did, but remember – there's NO RIGHT OR WRONG! The only way
for the audience to believe that you messed up is if
you indicate to them that you THINK you messed
up. If you stand there confidently, they'll think that
you meant to do whatever you did, and most likely
they'll think you're a genius.

∪∩∪∩∪∩∪

---

8. Go back to step 1, and play the next track of emotional music.

This is a great exercise to get you listening to the emotion of
music and translating it to a character. Although the music itself
won't change when you re-listen to it, you can do this exercise over
and over again; simply discover new situations for new characters
each time you do it. When you add words, you can try focusing on
images one time, or on internal emotions the next time, or your
childhood that led you to this place, etc., etc. See what's easier for you
when it comes to the words you sing. Is it easier for you to sing about
the emotions you're feeling or the things you're seeing or metaphors
or what?

I don't care how much experience you have doing musical improv or songwriting – *anyone* can do this exercise and do it really well. If you want to do this exercise with different music, try going to You Tube and searching for "emotional instrumental music" or "angry instrumental music" or even just "instrumental music" – there's some really weird stuff, but you can do this exercise to it!

To summarize, the steps are:

1. Listen to the music and its emotion

2. Feel the emotion

3. Show the emotion

4. Move in that emotion

5. Vocalize (no words) in that emotion to the music

6. Plant yourself and sing words, and

7. End when the music ends.

Play TRACKS 2-6 and do Exercise 1 now.

Fabulous. I hope you had fun doing that. If you didn't, you were probably thinking way too hard. Try it again and don't put so much pressure on yourself – have a blast!

♪ ♪ ♪

Chapter 2
Melody 101

I like to begin with melody, because it's the most overlooked part of musical improv. We tend to get so preoccupied with the lyrics and rhyming, we end up singing along on one note. It gets boring pretty quickly for the listener. If there's no melody, then your lyrics had better be brilliant, because that's the only thing the audience can focus on. On the other hand, if you have a nice melody, the audience will listen to that and not put so much emphasis on your words.

It's like doing a regular non-musical improv scene. There, the default of the improviser is to just stand and talk (called a "talking head scene" by most improvisers.) This is boring for the audience to watch – you BETTER be witty or brilliant, because there's not much else to watch in the scene. You COULD have a wonderful location, where you interact with objects to SHOW how you feel, or to symbolize a relationship or situation in your character's life.

Same with the one-note melody. If you're just standing on one note, there's nothing else to hear other than the words, so they better be stellar, since that's the only thing the audience is focused on. As opposed to having a melody, which can express what your character is feeling and going through with NO words, if desired.

Play and listen to TRACK 7 now.

The sentence is sung at first in an extremely typical improv manner! The second way is much more enjoyable to listen to – and more fun to sing!

It's doubly hard because so much modern music really has very little melody. So my younger students naturally sing like they're used to hearing – one note. Stop it right now. Sing with a nice melody, and your songs will be ten times better than the average Joe Improviser and songwriter.

Simply put, the melody is how slowly or quickly the notes go up and down. You can picture the shape of a melody as a line. A melody that's all on one note is a straight horizontal line. A melody that slowly and evenly goes up would be a diagonal line, lower on the left than the right. The line would fall sharply if the note jumped down. You can see the line if you look at the melody notes on sheet music. And you can hear it as well.

Frè - re   Jac - ques,   Frè - re   Jac - ques,   dor - mez vous?   Dor - mez vous?

Did you know: There are an infinite number of unique melodies?

Exercise 2 – Making Up Different Melodies

(My thanks to Steve Gilbane of ImprovBoston for this and the next exercise.)

The piano will play the same eight beats of music over and over. Fill each eight beats with a melody.

No words for now – just sing on a "la la."

Try not to have more than two consecutive notes be the same, just to practice moving around melodically.

After hearing the first eight beats (you have to listen to the music before you start singing!), fill in each line (eight beats) with a different melody. Have fun. Try long slow notes, or quick ones. Try a melody that goes up, and one that goes down. And one that goes up and then down…oh, you get the idea.

I'll give you the beats, at first. The strongest beat is on the first beat of the eight. Another strong beat (but not as strong as the first, marks the downbeat of the next measure – so you'll hear a background beat of 1 2 3 4 5 6 7 8. Be sure to keep your melodies within the eight beats, knowing that each line starts with the strong first beat. I'll drop the beats after several go-arounds, so you can practice hearing when each line starts on your own.

Draw the shape of the melodic line in the air with a finger simultaneously as you sing. I want you to get used to having and knowing the shape of your music, and it helps to hear it and SEE it. If your finger isn't going up or down, your melody is staying on the same note, and that can be boring!

Play TRACK 8 and do Exercise 2 now.

Exercise 2A – Five Beat Melody Lines

Most of you will have filled the entire 8 beats when you sing. That's natural – I said fill the 8 beats, so you probably started at beat one and sang until beat eight in each line.

> ◠◡◠◡◠◡◠
> YOU DON'T HAVE TO SING AND FILL EVERY
> MOMENT THAT THE MUSIC IS PLAYING!
> ◡◠◡◠◡◠◡

This is a huge point for many reasons...

* It will seem more like a real song if there are pauses (rests) within the melody/lyrics.

* Much beauty is found in the stillness and silence of a song.

* It gives the listener AND the singer a chance to hear and check back in with the music.

* If you're improvising, it gives you a chance to think of your upcoming rhymes/direction of the song.

Play Track 8 again, and improvise new melodies for each line, but this time only sing until beat five. (So you rest on beats 6,7, and 8.)

Play TRACK 8 and do exercise 2A now.

Exercise 2B – Various Melody Length Lines

Same as exercise 2A, but sing until beat 7, resting on beat 8. In fact, choose any number from 2-8 and fill THAT number of beats, resting until the end of the line. Sing that amount of beats for at least 4 lines before you switch to another number.

This will give you a good feeling of different ways to sing a line of melody. You don't have to automatically fall into the same kind of line for every song you do. It will also give you practice on hearing when lines start and end.

Play TRACK 8 and do Exercise 2B now.

Think of the Beatle's song "Ob-La-Di, Ob-La-Da". The chorus fills seven beats for the first line of the chorus, then five, then seven, then five. (The "Ob" and "La" of "Ob-La-Di" are pick up notes to the first down beat of "Di." Start counting the beats on the "Di.") Sing it and count out the beats, or if you don't know the song, find it on the internet and listen to the chorus (you know it's the chorus, because it has the title in it!) and count the beats. The 7,5,7,5 beat has a very natural feel.

Your songs will be much better if you learn the skill of this last exercise – namely, to know when musical lines begin and end, regardless of how many beats you fill per line.

Exercise 3 – Ear Training

While we're at it, let's do a little ear training, because you might want to pick up someone else's melody to sing a song together. (And you definitely want to listen to and repeat your OWN melody!)

Just like the last exercise, the piano will play eight beats of music over and over. One of our singers will fill in eight beats, and then YOU repeat what you just heard to fill in the next eight beats. Then another of us will sing a different eight beats of melody and you repeat that. And so on, and so on. You're just repeating what you've heard, in an octave that's comfortable for you.

Remember to draw the shape of your melodic line in the air with a finger.

Have fun!

Play TRACK 9 and do Exercise 3 now.

Exercise 4 - Melodies in a Full Verse

We'll be using the next few tracks for many different exercises. As you listen to the tracks, just make up a nice melody for each one. Don't use words for now. Focus on the melody and sing "la la" or "tee tee" or whatever floats your boat.

Remembering the first exercise we did, use the emotion/attitude that is in the music. Let me HEAR the emotion in your voice in how you sing your "la la las." An angry verse might have short staccato "La! Las!" or long, growly "Laaaaaaaas!" They will sound very different from a joyous verse of light "la la las!" or floaty "laaaaaaaaas." If I could see you, I'd want to see the emotion expressed in your entire body.

A Typical Verse
4 lines of 8 beats

Now, these tracks are single verses. A typical verse is four lines. A typical line is eight beats (two measures of quarter notes.) If it's a waltz, or a song with a 1-2-3, 1-2-3 beat, then there are typically four strong beats, or 12 regular beats, in a line. Track 15 has this kind of song.

When the music starts, it's important to listen to the introduction, to get the feel and style of the music – to get connected to it. I often see improvisers start singing as soon as the first note is struck, and am surprised that they would do such a thing. You wouldn't go out on stage in a non-musical scene and start speaking as soon as your scene partner opens his/her mouth. You want to hear what they are offering so you can respond appropriately. Same with musical improv. Your accompanist is an equal scene partner, and is offering you wonderful gifts. Listen to what he/she plays so you can respond appropriately. (And "appropriately" in this case is checking in with whatever the style of music evokes in you – so there is no wrong choice, as long as it's honest.)

The music doesn't stay on the same chord - there is a chord progression - so move with it. As I said, you've heard a lot of music in your life, so you know what sounds right or sounds off. Trust yourself.

The four lines of each verse should sound like they are in the same song. So if you sing the first line with long, slow notes, you'll want to continue that feel for the rest of the verse. You don't want to sing EXACTLY the same notes for each of the four lines (that would probably be a little boring.) Remember, the chords will change, so you have to go up or down with the music. Listen to the music and if you go along with it, your notes will change naturally.

The fourth line of each verse is going to end the verse. Depending on the song, it might sound like it's the ending (for you musicians, that means going back to the I or tonic), or it may sound like it's going someplace else, like to a chorus. Don't worry about the technicalities. Just go wherever the music goes.

Track 10 gives an example of a one-verse melody:

Play TRACK 10 now for an example.

Now play TRACKS 11-15, and do Exercise 4.

Go back and sing different melodies to those tracks. It might help to change the character or situation in your mind for the verses.

Also draw that melodic line in the air with your finger as you sing a couple of these verses again. Is your finger in one place, which means you're staying on one note too long? Remember to move that melody line. Are you tending to do the same kind of melodic line? If so, mix it up.

Remember, you're making this up – there IS no right or wrong thing to sing! (I'm trying to get you in good habits to guard against the pitfalls that all too many songwriters and improvisers fall into.) Think about that – there's no inherently right or wrong thing to sing. It's awesome! You can sing whatever you want, and it's right! Be free and sing what you feel in the music. Sing what you feel in your heart!

Exercise 5 – Putting Words With Melody

Now play those tracks 11-15 again. This time, hear the emotion and sing actual words.

Do NOT worry about rhyming.

As you listen to the introduction, again think who your character is, where you might be, and what the situation is. Sing the words about how you feel, what you see, your history, what the situation is – you know the drill.

You can sing about what your character feels, sees, hears, smells, and of course is thinking. What does your character want? What is he/she dreaming of? If you like similes or metaphors, use those! Whatever! Just sing words in the emotion of the music. In fact, exaggerate the emotion – the words will come easier.

Again, do not worry about rhyming yet. Just sing words that match what your character is experiencing and wants.

Remember to move the melody line!!

You can play the same tracks many times. Although it evokes the same emotion in you, change the situation for your character (the Who, What, and Where – or as we at Zenprov like to say, the "CORE" – Character, Objective, Relationship, Environment) so different lyrics are appropriate.

Play TRACKS 11-15 and do Exercise 5 now.

Excellent! Now that you (hopefully!) have the feel of the music being reflected in a moving melody line, let's move on to rhyming and lyrics, shall we?

♪ ♪ ♪

Chapter 3
Lyrics and Rhyming 101

Rhyming Basics

After teaching this for twenty years, I'm always surprised at the range of knowledge when it comes to rhyming. Some people can rhyme innately. Others barely understand the concept and struggle mightily. Even if you're good at rhyming, you might not know some of the finer points or names for certain things, so let's all get on the same page.

1. Two words rhyme when the ACCENTED SYLLABLE onward sound the same.

> Béar
> Cháir
>
> Flóor
> Whóre
>
> Swéater
> Bétter

Illégal
Béagle

Pórtable
Affórdable

2. Rhymes are based on SOUND, not spelling.

It doesn't matter how a word is spelled, as long as they sound the same. "Turn" and "fern" rhyme because they SOUND the same. It doesn't matter that one is "urn" and one is "ern." The above example of portable and affordable is another example. Not spelled the same, but since most people pronounce "portable" as "pordable," it sounds like "affordable," so they rhyme. Along the same lines, just because it's spelled the same, doesn't mean it rhymes. "Bone" and "one" do NOT rhyme!

3. Know your Masculine and Feminine Rhymes.

A **masculine** rhyme only has to rhyme **one syllable** (think, "Men are simple." "Yeah, they sure....Hey!") as in:

best, and
pest

Feminine rhymes have **more than one syllable** to rhyme (think, "Women are complicated and hard." "Yeah, they sure...whaaa?") as in:

Pickle, and
tickle

It doesn't matter how many syllables the word has – it's from the accented syllable onwards. So...

dart, and
fart   is a masculine rhyme.

wiggle, and
giggle   is a feminine rhyme.

Cabaret and
fey?   is a ….?

Remember, it's from the accented syllable on, so even though "cabaret" is three syllables long, the accent is on its last syllable. So it's a masculine rhyme. Having multi-syllabic masculine rhymes makes it seem much harder than it is. You're only rhyming one sound, but because there are more syllables, it makes you seem smarter!

4. The consonant sound before the accented syllable(s) must be different.

Rhymes are entirely based on sounds.

bear, and
bare

…is not a rhyme because it's the exact SAME sound. They are the same word, "rhymically" (is that a word?!) speaking. If you use homonyms (that's what "bear" and "bare" are), the audience will feel let down when they hear the falsely rhyming word. They won't really know why, but there will be a deflation after their anticipation of what you will come up with. (It's the same disappointment when the improviser or song-writer uses the exact same word to rhyme with itself. Don't laugh – I've heard it plenty of times in shows and in actual written songs!)

5. Rhyme schemes are designated by letters.

The rhyme word at the end of the first line of a song or poem is represented by a lower case "a." Any line that ends with a rhyme of that word will end with an "a." If the next line ends with a new sounding word, it's designated a "b," and any words that rhyme with THAT word are a "b". Then "c," then "d," and so on, and so on.

If I asked you to sing an **aabb** rhyme scheme, that means I would want the first two lines to rhyme, and then the second two lines to rhyme with a new rhyme.

> My little old man and I fell **out**;   a
> I'll tell you what 'twas all **about**,--   a
> I had money and he had <u>none</u>,   b
> And that's the way the noise <u>begun</u>.   b
>   - Mother Goose, "The Quarrel"

Here's an **abab** rhyme scheme:

> All are architects of **Fate**   a
> Working in these walls of <u>Time</u>;   b
> Some with massive deeds and **great**   a
> Some with ornaments of <u>rhyme</u>.   b
>   - Henry Wadsworth Longfellow, "The Builders," 1850

Limericks are a form you should be familiar with. If you're really good at writing them, you may want to try song verses in this style, if the musician is playing a waltz. The third and fourth lines of the limerick would make up one line in a song, since they are half as long as the other lines. That gives you an internal rhyme, which is very cool! Here's a classic limerick, which most of us have heard:

> A wonderful bird is the **pelican,**   a
> His bill will hold more than his **belican**,   a
> He can take in his <u>beak</u>   b
> Enough food for a <u>week</u>   b
> But I'm damned if I see how the **helican**!   a
>   - Dixon Lanier Merritt, 1910

(Ooh, saucy language from over a century ago!)

Here is a sonnet, which is 14 lines in iambic pentameter:

Shall I compare thee to a summer's **day**?	a
Thou art more lovely and more <u>temperate</u>:	b
Rough winds do shake the darling buds of **May**,	a
And summer's lease hath all too short a <u>date</u>:	b
Sometime too hot the eye of heaven *shines*,	c
And often is his gold complexion **dimmed**;	d
And every fair from fair sometimes *declines*,	c
By chance, or nature's changing course **untrimmed;**	d
But thy eternal summer shall not <u>fade</u>,	e
Nor lose possession of that fair thou *owest*,	f
Nor shall death brag thou wander'st in his <u>shade</u>,	e
When in eternal lines to time thou *growest*;	f
So long as men can breathe, or eyes can **see**,	g
So long lives this, and this gives life to **thee**.	g

- William Shakespeare, "Sonnet 18," 1609

᭦᭦᭦᭦᭦᭦

Did you know? Pairs of lines of any length rhyming
aa bb cc are called couplets. (Couple? Couplet? Get it?)
The lines themselves must be the same length.

᭦᭦᭦᭦᭦᭦

6. Don't forget False, Slant, Approximate, Near or "Nashville" rhymes.

My partner, Marshall Stern, was a songwriter in Nashville for many years, and he calls these "Nashville rhymes" because they're so pervasive there. These are rhymes that aren't exact, but they're close to rhymes. They fool the ear enough that we think they're rhymes, and they tend to be enjoyable to the audience because they are unexpected. But if they're too far off base, the audience won't accept them as rhymes and will be disappointed.

Approximate rhymes often are assonants. Whereas **rhyme** is a similarity of vowel AND consonant ("bake" and "cake"), **assonance** is a similarity of vowel sounds ("bake" and "late.")

> His hound is to the hunting **gane**,
> His hawk to fetch the wild-fowl **hame**,
> His lady's **ta'en** another **mate**
> So we **may mak** our dinner sweet
> - Unknown, "Twa Corbies" (1611)

Hmmm. It gives us pause. See? Even unknown people of long ago were writing songs with false rhymes! The more things change, the more things stay the same – the lyrics of many current rap songs are littered with approximate/false/half rhymes!

7. Be Creative.

Your creativity can really shine, especially with multi-syllabic (feminine) rhymes. Cole Porter was great at this. In his song "Brush Up Your Shakespeare" from Kiss Me Kate, he rhymes "Othella" with "fella" and "Flatter 'er" (flatter her) with "Cleopatterer." These rhymes are exact rhymes, as they are written/sang, but only because Porter was very creative and changed the pronunciation or the actual word. ("Cleopatterer" instead of "Cleaopatra" to rhyme with "flatter 'er.")

In the song "You Could Drive a Person Crazy" from Company, Stephen Sondheim, a master rhymer, rhymes:

"When a person's personality is personable"

with the line:

"It's harder than a matador coercin' a bull"

You read that right! "Personable" and "coercin' a bull!

These kinds of rhymes are very creative and are unexpected, which makes them very enjoyable for the listener. I know I find it a bummer when listening to music if I know exactly what the end of the line is going to be before the singer gets there. In my old ImprovBoston days, when doing improvised Blues, we would indicate a big old rhyming train coming down the tracks if someone was doing an obvious setup.

These types of rhymes can be great because they are unexpected and creative, but if you are sharing lines and setting someone up for a rhyme, you should use an exact rhyme, or as exact as you can make it!

More sophisticated musical improv audiences will be disappointed in obvious rhymes, but most are just thrilled you're up there singing! Don't worry about being clever as you start – just keep rhyming.

If you're fairly new to the rhyming thing, you may want to keep to the simple masculine rhymes (be, tea) at first, then challenge yourself to put those kind of rhymes in creative context (i.e. in West Side Story, one of the characters, in describing his delinquent-producing home life, says that his Mother is an "S.O.B." and that his Grandmother "pushes tea." Still very simple rhymes, but "pushing tea" is a very unexpected phrase using the word "tea.") Then challenge yourself to rhyme more complex, feminine words.

Rhyming actually gets easier, the more you do it! So practice, practice, practice!

Let's Rhyme!

Let's just jump in, shall we? You've really got to warm up your brain-mouth connection in order to think up and sing lyrics quickly. Let's start with the word association exercise again.

Exercise 6 – Word Association

I had you do this exercise during the "Before You Start" portion of this book, but let's do it again. If you have someone to do it with, fabulous. But you can definitely play with yourself. (Insert leering chuckle here.)

Do this exercise aloud. Again, we're not just warming up the brain, but the brain-mouth connection, which you don't get if you just make a list in your head.

Say the first word that comes into your mind, and then say a word which directly relates to that word. (It doesn't have to make sense to anyone else!) And so on and so on.

Beware of lists in this exercise. Sometimes you'll want lists in your songs, but that's not this exercise. If you find yourself on a list, BREAK IT! For example, you might find yourself just listing colors ("orange, yellow, red, blue, green...") This is almost mindless, and isn't really warming up your intellect. Break the pattern as soon as you can. For example: (Aloud) "Orange, yellow..." – "Oops," you say to yourself, "This is a list! Let me break it and associate differently with the last word said." (Aloud) "Yellow, SUN, moon, butt..." etc.

Do Exercise 6 now.

Exercise 7 – Rhyme Association

Let's give a little twist to this last exercise. This time, say a word out loud. ("Butt.") Now say a word that rhymes with that word. ("Mutt.") Now associate with that word. ("Dog.") Now rhyme with THAT word. ("Fog.") It's very simple...

Just rhyme, associate, rhyme, associate, rhyme, etc...

Example:

Butt → mutt
   ↓
   dog → fog
      ↓
      grey → day
         ↓
         hot → pot
            ↓
            high → sigh
               ↓
               depression → regression
                  ↓
                  child → wild

Please realize it's up to you how hard it is. I'm starting the exercises off pretty easy, since this is Rhyming 101, but try more complicated rhymes, if you wish.

You WILL get much better and faster as you practice!

Do Exercise 7 now.

Exercise 8 – Easy Masculine Rhymes

Rhyme the following masculine rhymes, first with as many one-syllable words as you can, then continue rhyming with as many multi-syllabic words as you can think of.

Example: **Red**

One syllable rhymes	Multi-syllabic Rhymes
bed	ahead
dead	behead
fed	embed
head	instead
lead	misled
Ned	unwed
ped	widespread
said	biomed
Ted	overfed
wed	overhead
bled	thoroughbred
fled	infrared
pled	pudding head
sled	
bread	
dread	
Fred	
tread	
shed	
shred	
spread	

You can see MY rhyming process here – when I'm looking for simple rhymes, I tend to go through the alphabet, and then try blends of _L, _R, _H and STR, and SHR words! I even know I missed a bunch, but these were ones that came right away.

And as for the multi-syllabic list, notice I have "pudding head" in there. That's technically the "head" rhyme with an adjective in front of it. But it seems like a multi-syllabic word because the two words really are used together as an expression unto itself. This is a great way to make a masculine rhyme seem more difficult, without hardly any extra work! "Banana bread," "pencil lead," "talking head" – so many possibilities!

Now you try with these:

Day

Seat

Dish

Cat

Do Exercise 8 now.

Exercise 9 – Seemingly Harder Masculine Rhymes

Turning a masculine rhyme into a feminine rhyme is easy and seems much harder than it is. Which is always great for improvisers. Let the audience think you are freakin' brilliant – only you (and everyone who reads this book) will know differently!

Simply rhyme the adjective before the noun. (Sondheim does this all the time!)

Example:

Bad cat (stressing the "bad" – as if I'm saying it was a bad cat as opposed to a good cat. Not a bad cat as opposed to a bad dog – that would be stressing the "cat.")

<u>Rhymes</u>
Sad cat
Mad cat
Glad cat
Fad cat
Dad cat
Rad cat

Now you practice this and rhyme these words…

Blue dog

Green job

Light load

You can also rhyme complicated words by breaking them down into smaller words – see Rhyming Basic #7 on being creative…

Do Exercise 9 now.

Exercise 10 – Easier Feminine Rhymes

Remember, rhyming is from the accented syllable on, so for a feminine rhyme, you have at least two syllables to deal with. Here's an example:

Ocean	→	Lotion
		Motion
		Notion
		Potion
		Commotion
		Devotion
		Locomotion
		Sales promotion

Now you try these:

Honey

Power

Crazy

Drama

Innovation

If you're in a tight spot and have a difficult word to rhyme, like "Unsubstantially," many improvisers will just rhyme the last syllable, "ly." I suppose you could say it's technically cheating, but it's okay if you have to. The audience will think it's okay. But nowhere NEAR as rewarding as if you found some way to rhyme it properly!

Do Exercise 10 now.

Exercise 11 – Seemingly Harder Feminine Rhymes

Just like when we turned the masculine rhymes into feminine rhymes by rhyming the adjective before the final noun, we can make a feminine rhyme seem more complicated by doing the same thing. Simply have a feminine adjective to rhyme, instead of a one-syllable masculine adjective. (This is really what Sondheim does!)

Example:
A *Loquacious* kitten
A *bodacious* kitten
A *Vivacious* kitten

If you're really good at rhyming, you could rhyme both the words:
A *salacious mitten*

What the hell is a salacious mitten? I don't know – but it works!

Now try these, rhyming the italicized words:

> *Knowing* rhymes
>
> *Pretty* piggy
>
> *Ostentatious* verse
>
> *Amusing* balloons
>
> *Dating* a caveman

> **Do Exercise 11 now.**

♪ ♪ ♪

Chapter 4
Musical Games 101

These are some simple musical improv games that require no to low singing talent. It's lovely during an improv show to add variety (whether in short-form shows or long-form shows) by adding music. These games are mostly used in short-form shows, but can definitely be adapted to fit into a long-form show. The singing games in this section can be done with simple rhyming, and most give you the melody line, so you don't even have to make one up! I'm doing these first because the singers only have to sing one word or line at a time, which seems a good place to start. But just because they are simple doesn't mean they are always easy! Have fun!

Dance Based/No Singing

Ballet

You can take a suggestion of a historical event (like the moon landing) or a well-known nursery rhyme, fairy tale or even a well-known story (like The Wizard of Oz). You simply replay the story, with people playing the characters and objects in the story. The musician plays very classical sounding music (or if you don't have a musician, you can play some classical music over the sound system), and you act out the story with all the ballet-typical posturing and moves. (standing on tip-toes, leaping, spins, lifting each other, pointed toes, long necks, etc.) Watch some ballet to really get the style and moves down. You CAN play it really badly, with winking at the audience at how you're so bad the entire time you're dancing. Many people do that because they are self-conscious of how little they know ballet, and want the audience to know that THEY know that they suck. Personally, I prefer watching improvisers dance as well as they can, with the attitude that they are the most amazing ballet artists in the world. After all, that's the attitude of real ballet dancers, so it's in style. Otherwise, you're sort of apologizing ahead of time (and during!) the performance. It's the same when you improvise a song or a scene or do any sort of performing. Why apologize for it, especially when there IS no right or wrong?!

I've also performed this as a guessing game, where an improviser OR an audience member guesses what the event or story is!

Modern Dance

Very similar to "Ballet," but it's done in – surprise! – the style of Modern or Interpretive dance. You can get a similar input of some kind of story, or just get a concept or word, and do an interpretive dance. You can add vocals/words if you wish, which can be sung or just spoken.

Performance Art

This structure can use accompaniment, but does not need it. This can be one big performance art piece, like modern/interpretive dance, or, the way I learned it, having three actors portray three different performance artists. A host welcomes the audience to whatever location (i.e. the Velvet Pillow Lounge at the Highway 41 Holiday Inn) and the event (for Wednesday Local Artist Night) and has the artists introduce themselves. The performance artists should be varied – one might be a wacky artsy performance artist, another a children's book writer, another an opera singer or rap artist. The host gets a word or topic, and we see the artists' pieces on this topic.

Emotional Symphony

This structure needs no musical accompaniment. Four to Twenty actors can play this game. If you have a lot of improvisers, you group them into sections, like a real orchestra, with each section taking an emotion. Otherwise, each person gets an emotion from the audience. Try to make sure they are varied, and not "mad" "pissed" "angry" or all negative or of the same ilk. The actors can just use sounds of their emotions, or can add words, to make it a bit of a rant type of game.

The conductor conducts, making it clear who s/he is pointing to, indicating when to get louder and more intense, and when to get softer/less intense. The conductor usually starts out giving focus to one person/section at a time, but can get more complex, making two, three, or more people/sections sound at a time, and having some be loud and others soft in juxtaposition to each other. Big finish. (Often using the funniest emotion as a little capper at the end.)

Simple Singing Games

Dr. Know-It-All Song

You probably know the game Dr. Know-It-All, where (usually three) improvisers stand or sit shoulder to shoulder and answer a question from the audience one – word – at – a – time. This is the same, but the improvisers sing. You don't even have to rhyme, but it's friggin' amazing if you can!

This song can be the end of a Dr. K structure (after answering questions, the host pimps the doctor into singing – usually just a verse), or it can be an entire structure unto itself.

This is a very simple concept, but can be hard to accomplish well. Practice and have super fun!

Da Doo Ron Ron

This game is based on the 1963 hit single "Da Doo Ron Ron" by The Crystals. The song was written by Jeff Barry, Ellie Greenwich and Phil Spector. Look it up on the internet to hear how the actual song goes.

This musical game is usually played with four or more improvisers. It's often played as an elimination game, and I know I've played it many times with chosen audience members getting up, and singing in competition with the professional improvisers.

The singers should stand in a row across the stage. The usual first "get" (suggestion) from the audience is a simple one-syllable first name. Say it's "Hank." The first person ends their line with the suggestion, then the game is to just rhyme with that until someone can't think of any more rhymes. Every third person has to do THREE rhymes, just to keep it interesting.

So if you have four people up on stage for this structure, it could look something like this:

(The words in italics are sung by everybody, including the audience.)

Person 1:   .   I met him on a Friday and his name was **Hank.**

Everybody: *Da doo ron-ron-ron, Da doo ron-ron*

Person 2:   He was a crummy teller at a crappy **bank.**

Everybody: *Da doo ron-ron-ron, Da doo ron-ron*

Person 3:   (*Yeah*) He drove a **tank.**

                (*Yeah*) He really **stank.**

                (*Yeah*) He gave me a check that was **blank.**

Everybody:	*Da doo ron-ron-ron, Da doo ron-ron*
Person 4:	He left out some meat and it was really **rank.**
Everybody:	*Da doo ron-ron-ron, Da doo ron-ron*
Person 1:	When he broke up with me, my heart just **sank.**
Everybody:	*Da doo ron-ron-ron, Da doo ron-ron*
Person 2:	(*Yeah*) He tried to **spank,**
	(*Yeah*) But I just **shrank,**
	(*Yeah*) So he gave it a **yank.**

Okay. You make up your own rules about what is acceptable – so that last racy rhyme might eliminate that singer! Generally, a person is out of the game if s/he hesitates too long, repeats a rhyme (sometimes it's fun to argue with the host/referee – "But I said the European "Banque" with a "que!" not the American "k!"), or makes up a word and is caught at it. The host/ref makes the final call on what's acceptable, but it's always nice to have the audience vote, if it's a close call.

Also, as with ANY competitive improv (and I've done a ton of it all over the world!), it's a competition for SHOW ONLY! The competition is only the fun packaging that gets the audience involved. You gotta know how to realistically get "out" in such games – it's about the timing, or feeling the beats in any given structure. There's nothing worse than one of these games going on and on until it's boring. ESPECIALLY when you are playing with audience members. It's very nice when an audience member beats the professionals, although please make it realistic when you get out, because obviously "throwing the game" in favor of the audience is stinky. When they feel they really have beaten the professionals, it's energizing for them and the whole show.

When playing with audience members, you could skip the three-rhyme line to make it easier if you want, and just have all regular length lines.

A nice way to increase the tension, and therefore the excitement of the game, is after each person gets out, the suggestion gets harder – "Let's have a two-syllable first name!" "Now a three-syllable first name!" – and the pace gets faster. (Try rhyming "Chesterfield" at a really quick pace!)

Warning: The audience WILL shout out "Chuck" just to try to make you say the F-bomb. It's totally up to the style of your troupe if you want to do that or not.

I did have a practice track, but since this is an actual written and published song, I don't have the rights to give the audio out. You CAN play this game a cappella (without musical accompaniment), or find a karaoke version to practice to.

Doo Wah Diddy

This game is based on the song "Doo Wah Diddy" made popular by Manfred Mann in 1964. Again, I recommend listening to the song at least once, so you know what you're parodying.

Seem similar to *Da Doo Ron Ron*? It should - *Doo Wah Diddy* was written in the same year by the same composers! I always get these two games mixed up, since they're so similar!

Just like in *Da Doo Ron Ron*, you line up across stage, and instead of getting a name as the suggestion, get any word (an object, something you'd find in your car, something in your kitchen – be prepared to rhyme "spatula," - etc.) Again, you can start out simple, with a one-syllable word and get harder as you go along. You can get audience members up on stage and play it as an elimination game, if you wish. This really is the same game as

Da Doo Ron Ron, but just a slightly different melody and non-sense syllables. Italicized words are sung by everybody.

So it might look like this if you got, say, "litter" for your input:

Person 1:	I went to the store and bought some cat **litter**
Everybody:	*Doo wah diddy diddy dum diddy doo*
Person 2:	I should spend some money and hire a pet **sitter**
Everybody:	*Doo wah diddy diddy dum diddy doo*
Person 3:	I'm not **bitter** (*I'm not bitter*)
	Or a **quitter** (*or a quitter*)
	I'm not bitter or a quitter, and that's what I wrote
	on my **Twitter**

Etc., etc. Whatever I said for Da Doo Ron Ron should apply.

Again, I don't have rights to give out audio to this actual song. Please try to find a karaoke version!

Make Up Your Own Nonsense Phrase Line Song

You can make up your own version of the two previous games. Get a nonsense phrase from the audience (I would shout out "wicky wicky wack wack woo," myself) and put it to a simple melody. Improvise your song a few times in rehearsal, so your entire troupe knows how the song melody goes. In the game introduction, get the phrase and then teach the audience how to sing it when it comes up. (Your musician can dictate right there how the phrase will go.) They'll pick it up quickly if you reference Doo wah Diddy and/or Da Doo Ron Ron in your intro.

Irish Drinking Song

Track 16 has four verses of The Irish Drinking Song music. (The fourth verse is really slow.) We'll make the melody really obvious so you can hear how it goes, and use a wood block sound (during the first verse only) where the rhymes go.

The suggestion I usually get for this game is a nasty habit, like picking your nose. You can also ask for an Irish name. Then, with all the singers standing in a row across the stage, each person takes one line of the four-line verse. At the end of the verse, everyone sings, "I-dee-I-dee-I-dee-I, dee-I-dee-I-dee-I!", during which the person at the extreme right (in spot #1) who started that verse, makes their way to the end of the line. So now the person who was in spot #2, is now in the first spot and starts the next verse.

This game usually goes for four or five verses. The first verse starts by introducing the main character of the song, something like, "There once was a lad name Sean who liked to pick his nose." Then it just tells the story of Sean and his horrible fate, which came from picking his nose. For the last verse, it's always great for the person who is in the #1 spot to start their line with, "So the moral of this story is..." blah blah blah blah blah!

For now, just concentrate on telling a story about this person who does this nasty habit.

Verses are just four typical lines, of two typical rhyming couplets:

Spot #1:	There once was a lad named Sean who liked to pick his **nose.**
Spot #2:	And he would pull the boogers out and wipe them on his **clothes**
Spot #3:	His pants were green, his shirt was green, and everything was <u>green,</u>
Spot #4:	And it was the foulest thing his mother ever <u>seen</u>!
All:	Oh, I-dee-I-dee-I-dee-I, dee-I-dee-I-dee-I!

It really helps to keep the story going if you make things happen. And personally, I think that it hurts the story to use first person. Watch saying "I" saw this or "I" thought that, or "I" did this and that. Keep it to the infamous story of the person – think of it as a story so astounding, that it's been told/sung about for generations.

To hear/practice this game, play TRACK 16.

Generic Line Musical Improv Games

You can make up your own musical line games like these by simply choosing a song style (see Appendix F) and singing one line at a time. Your musical director should be able to come up with a chord progression in that style. I do recommend going over the song at least a few times in rehearsal before doing it on stage, since you're all supposed to be singing the same melody.

You can choose a style and each singer can do one entire verse at a time, but I'll cover that in Musical Games 201, since you should be setting up your rhymes for that.

Part 2

Musical Improv 201
(Decent Level)

Chapter 5
Melody 201

Finding Melodies

Spoken words have a natural melody and rhythm. We don't speak like old-time robots, with every single syllable on one level, so why would we sing like that? Listen to the melody of a word. Say the word "chrysanthemum" out loud. Hear the rhythm? Chry – saaaan-the-mum. Short long short short. And the melody. Accented syllables usually are higher pitch. And if you listen closely, you'll hear the "mum" is lower than the "the." Chrysanthemum. (Unless you're from a weird part of the country, and have a weird, different accent than my absolutely normal and correct one!)

Now extrapolate a melody (and rhythm) from this. One that follows the natural melody and rhythm of the word. The notes can be subtle and go up and down just a little bit, or a lot. The short beats can be really short compared to the long, or just a bit shorter. Sing it a bunch of ways.

Remember, there is no right or wrong. It's up to you and your style!

You know who's great at following the natural melody and rhythm of words? Bruce Springsteen. Say "Born in the USA" out loud. You'll notice that the rhythm and melody of how you speak it is very similar to how he put it to music in his song of the same title. Say these phrases out loud:

"My Hometown"

"Glory Days"

"Pink Cadillac," and

"Born to Run."

Now listen to how Bruce puts them to music. He must have read this book!

Exercise 12 – Word Melodies

Practice speaking and then singing the following words and phrases. At first, as you read these words, say them out loud, and then come up with a sung melody for them a cappella (without instrumental music.)

Then you'll sing those words to Track 8.

Some people get this right away and can sing the word immediately. Others can't. If you feel like you're struggling with this and just "guessing" at what the natural rhythm and melody of a word is, then slow down, and speak the word once or twice. Then pretend you are saying the word, but say "da" for each syllable. Keep saying the word with "da" syllables. Slowing down will really let you hear the rhythm of the word more clearly. Hear each syllable and whether it is higher or lower than the preceding one. Eventually you'll get to a place where you can sing the phrase. Try singing it a few different ways. The more you practice, the easier it gets!

I'll give you an example of me doing "Chrysanthemum," at first with no music and then to Track 6. The last one I sing is an example of NOT following the natural rhythm and melody of the word. When you DO follow the natural rhythm and melody of words and phrases, it is said to "scan" well. That last example just doesn't scan.

Play TRACK 17 to hear my "chrysanthemum" example.

Try these words and phrases without the music. Say them out loud and get a solid rhythm and melody for each one.

Hello

Kumquats

Pancreas

How are you?

(depending on your meaning, this can be "How ARE you?" or "How are YOU?" – the meaning and the way you say it will change the melody.)

Filet Mignon

Alka-Seltzer

That was my toe.

Better turn the light on.

Nancy Howland Walker

He's a big bastard!

Oedipus schmoedipus

Wankel rotary engine.

Throatwobbler Mangrove

Underpants

Tuberculosis

He's going for it!

Scientific Method

Dizzy Dizzy Dinosaur

-Your Name-

Now that you've made up melodies, do it again, this time to music. Sing the word/phrase several times to the music, changing the intervals and rhythm to be more subtle or exaggerated versions of your original melody/rhythm. The melody will go up and down at the same points, but the intervals (how much they go up and down) will change, according to what the music is doing.

Play TRACK 8 and do Exercise 12.

Good. Now let's practice putting the natural melody of words to a full verse of music.

Exercise 13 – Word Melodies to Verse Music

Take some of the phrases from above and sing them to one of the Tracks 9-13. You can add words so it makes a little bit of sense (i.e., "Hello, I ate a kumquat. How are you?") It doesn't have to make much sense, but it should be more than just a list of words and phrases. Practice singing the melody of the actual words that you're saying.

If you can get into the habit of hearing the natural melody of words and actually singing them, you'll be different from the vast majority of improvisers who sing all on one note. It probably won't be a cohesive melody, but at least the melody line will be moving, which is good!

Play TRACKS 11-15 and do Exercise 13 now.

Fabulous! Now that you can find melodies for words, let's practice finding words for melodies…

Exercise 14 – Verse Melody with Words

Remember the exercise where we just did a full verse of melody on "La la?" Well, we're going to do something similar, and then add words to go along with the new melodies.

Tracks 18-22 have two verses of a song in a row. For each track, I want you to follow these steps.

1. Listen to the musical intro and get a feel for the style/emotion.

2. For the first verse, sing a melody line on "La la" (or "Doo be doo," etc.) which shows your emotion/attitude and actually moves up and down (no one-note melodies!)

3. Make sure the verse sounds like it goes together – that it's all from the same song (like my example on Track 10.)

4. Make sure the last (4th) line in the first verse feels like the end of the verse. (Again, like my example on Track 10.)

5. Now the music continues with the second verse. Try to keep as closely as possible to the melody you just sang in the first verse, but this time sing actual words. It doesn't have to rhyme. It can, but don't get all up in your head about it. The words don't even have to make complete sense. It's more important to just practice putting words and melody together.

You can also do this exercise to TV themes which have no lyrics - sing words that fit the melody and rhythm to "Bonanza" or "Star Trek!"

Many musical improv students are fine when they sing a melody with "la las," but as soon as they start singing words, the melody disappears. The last exercise, where you were singing words to their natural melody and thus moving the melody line, and this exercise help bridge the gap between great melody with no words, and great words with no melody.

Play TRACKS 18-22 and do Exercise 14 now.

♪ ♪ ♪

Chapter 6
Lyrics and Rhyming 201

We've practiced singing rhyming lines. If we just did that, the audience would be happy. Heck, they can't imagine themselves getting up and singing and rhyming in front of others, so you're already an amazing hero to them.

There is a secret to doing great improv songs, however, which will BLOW THE AUDIENCE AWAY! Very simply, it's setting up your rhymes. Or, to put it mathematically,

Set up Rhymes = BLOW AUDIENCE AWAY!

"Setting up rhymes" means that you actually think backwards, thinking of your important/funny word first, and then thinking of a rhyme for it. You sing the rhyme first and the important/funny word last.

It's like any type of comedy – you set up your joke and then – boom! – deliver the punchline. I'll call the important/funny word that you land on – the "landing word." I was going to call it the "punch word," but that suggests that it needs to be funny, which it doesn't. It's just the word or phrase that has to do with the topic being sung about.

Blah blahblahblah blah blah setup rhyme   A
Blah blahblah blah blahblah landing word   A

Setting up your rhymes is important not only for short-form musical improv funny verses, but for long-form shows. If you are forward rhyming, (singing a line and then coming up with the next line/rhyme) and singing how you'll be happy now, you might very well end up singing that you're in love with a cow, just to find a rhyme for the word "now." That can be fine for short-form, where the song might not have any connection to anything else, but if you're trying to tell a story, it can really derail the scene and even the show.

Setting up Rhymes Step by Step

Remember the exercise we did early on, when we said a word out loud, rhymed it, then associated, then rhymed and then associated? Like...

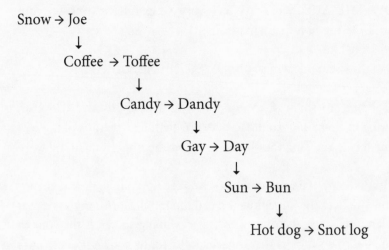

Snow → Joe
    ↓
    Coffee → Toffee
        ↓
        Candy → Dandy
            ↓
            Gay → Day
                ↓
                Sun → Bun
                    ↓
                    Hot dog → Snot log

Well, if you can do that, you can reverse rhyme!

Finding Good Words/Rhymes

Exercise 15 – Topic Word Association

Go down the list of topics I give below – for each one, think of a word or phrase really quickly that associates in that topic. For example, if the topic is "Improv," I might really quickly associate "Yes, And."

Here is your list of topics…

Improv

Summer

School

Politics

Chocolate

Taxes

Ice Cream

Driving

Environment

Do Exercise 15 now.

Okay, now let's look at the words you are associating in a topic. If you haven't guessed, these topics are like any suggestion you elicit from an audience for an improvised song. In fact, I remember singing many blues to the above topics!

Most of us do improv comedy, so we like our songs to be funny. That means you need funny words/concepts for your song. Even if your goal isn't comedy, you'll want your songs to be unique and memorable. Remember what your words were from Exercise 15, when you associated one word per topic? Were they bland, common words? Or were they unusual and uncommon words?

For example, if you were on the topic "summer" and said "sun," I would say that that is a fairly bland, common word. Whereas "melanoma," although a bit edgy, is certainly unexpected, and gives a better punch for a set up rhyme.

Exercise 16 – Unexpected Word Association

Do Exercise 15 again and come up with one unusual, unexpected, uncommon, visually interesting, poetic, or funny word for each topic.

Do Exercise 16 now.

Exercise 17 – Topic and Rhyme Association List

Just for practice, list as many associations for each topic as possible.

Do Exercise 17 now.

Now we're going to practice putting those words at end of sentences or phrases.

Exercise 18 – Using Rhyme Words in Sentences

Pick one of the topics from Exercise 15, or choose one of your own. Lightly slap your thigh (snap your fingers, tap your foot… whatever) to keep time to a one one thousand, two one thousand, three one thousand, four one thousand count. Most song lines are eight beats – we're doing four beats for this exercise. You're going to fill the first four beats with words, ending with the rhyme to your associated word. You'll fill the second four beats, ending with your associated word (the landing word).

Remember, you're thinking of the associated word first, then rhyming that word. You'll end your FIRST line of the couplet with the rhyme, and the SECOND line of the couplet with the important landing word.

For example, if the topic is "summer," I first think of my unusual associated word ("melanoma") and then come up with a rhyme for that word ("Roma"). So I might make a couplet like…

Last SUMmer I vaCAtioned on the BEAches near old **ROma**
(setup rhyme)

I GOT too much SUN and deVEloped **melaNOma**
(landing word)

(Capitalized syllables are the stressed beats when I slap/snap/tap.)

If you're not used to setting up your rhymes, you'll probably be a little slower. This is absolutely normal. The more you practice rhyming, the faster you will get at rhyming. The more you practice backwards thinking/setting up your rhymes, the faster you will get at setting up your rhymes. If you find this exercise too fast for you, simply put in four beats of rests in between each line. (Fill the first four beats with words, putting that setup rhyme word on the fourth beat. Rest for the next four beats. Then fill the third set of four beats with words, putting the important punch word on the fourth beat. End with four beats with no words.)

Done slower, the earlier example I gave would be…

> Last SUMmer I vaCAtioned on the BEAches near old ROma
> [REST]   [REST]   [REST]   [REST]
> I GOT too much SUN and deVEloped melaNOma
> [REST]   [REST]   [REST]   [REST]

The only reason I suggested having you filling 4 beats instead of 8, is that it's practice for rhyming, and I want you to be able to rhyme quickly just in case the song calls for it. If you can rhyme really quickly, then you should have no problem slowing down during a song.

Since song lines are usually eight beats, putting in an extra four beats in between the (four beat) lines in this exercise just makes it like a real song line length. I would much rather have you insert the four beats and rest in time to the beat, than trying to rush while you're not comfortable, TRYING to put words to every line, but sometimes slowing down or pausing or stopping because it's just too fast for you. The beat should be consistent, and shouldn't speed up or slow down.

Do as many couplets as you can in each topic. Always make sure you save your landing word for the SECOND line. You DO NOT want to be a "peak too sooner" and say it in your first line! (Peaking too soon is disappointing for all involved!) If you find yourself putting your important landing word first, then slow down, focus on setting up the word and then following through, and make sure you're resting for four beats between lines.

Do Exercise 18 now.

Good. You know you can make up lyrics and set up rhymes in a given beat. Now you're going to do the same thing, but this time to music.

Exercise 19 – Setting Up Rhymes to Music

Play Track 8. You'll notice that the eight beats are probably faster than the eight beats you just tapped out for the last exercises. That's okay. Pick a topic from Exercise 15 or from the Topic List in Appendix D, and just fill each eight beats with sung words. Wait, I take that back. Each eight beats is a line – you don't have to fill the ENTIRE eight beats with words – remember, rests and silences are wonderful in music. But it's important to know how long a line is and to keep it consistent through the song. So even if you stop singing before the eighth beat, don't start the second line until the next eight beat line starts. Or, if it's just going a bit too fast for you, do what we did in the last exercise. Sing one line (eight beats), rest for a line, sing the next line, rest for a line.

Remember to sing a melody (no one-note melodies!), and to SET UP YOUR RHYMES! Since it's the same music over and over, vary your melody with each new couplet.

Play TRACK 8 and do Exercise 19 now.

Exercise 20 – Setting up Rhymes in Verses

Now that you've mastered Track 8, play Tracks 11-15, which are normal verses. Pick a topic from the Topic List. You'll need AT LEAST one associated landing word and one rhyme word. This would be if you are singing the following rhyme scheme:

a
b
c
b

where B is the rhyme word and the associated landing word.

If that's not a problem for you, then get two associated words and sing two couplets for the verse. You'll probably sing this rhyme scheme:

a
a
<u>*b*</u>
<u>**b**</u>

This is the most common rhyme scheme for improvised songs, since most improvisers think it's easier to remember what they're rhyming.

As you start, make sure you're setting up your rhymes and singing a melody that sounds like the four lines go together. Listen to the music – go with the music when the chords change. And make sure the last line follows the music. Everything we've been learning is starting to come together!

Try different rhyme schemes...

a
<u>*b*</u>
a
<u>**b**</u>

This is a really enjoyable rhyme scheme. By not rhyming the second line to the first, you set up a tension that is satisfied once the rhyme does come. And it is easier than you think.

When doing the **aabb** or **abab** rhyme scheme, it's better if you can use the stronger of the two landing words for the B rhyme. End as strongly as you can! Don't sweat it and get all in your head wondering which is the better word – sometimes you just know that one of your concepts/words is way better. So save it so you can really stick that landing!

Play TRACKS 11-15 and do Exercise 20 now.

Exercise 21 – Ah Yes, I Remember It Well

Many years ago, I was driving in a car with Randy Craig, and somehow we were listening to the song "Ah Yes, I Remember it Well," from the musical *Gigi*, written by Alan Jay Lerner and Frederick Loewe. Randy said that it would be a great exercise, and it became one! Many thanks to Randy for this gem.

This is a great exercise for setting up rhymes. I usually play it with one other person, or in a circle, with each person taking a line. But you can certainly do it by yourself.

The conceit is that one person is misremembering things and the other is correcting him, and it's based on opposites or very close associations. So if it's two people, here's how it goes…

Person 1: Say any short statement. If you keep it in the past tense, it's a little easier, but it's not necessary. For example:

"I sat on a chair."

Person 2: Simply "correct" that statement by doing an opposite or association like:

"You stood on the **floor.**"

Person 1: You want Person 2 to rhyme with "floor," so first you think of a rhyme with "floor" and then come up with a line that will get Person 2 to say the word that you're thinking. You want to do it with a clear, short statement, hopefully using an opposite or close association. For example, if I want Person 2 to say the word "more" I think of an opposite/association, like "less" and use it in a short statement...

"I wanted *less.*"

Person 2: Has the word "floor" in her head, and so knows that "less" is either associated or opposite of a "floor" rhyme

"You wanted **more.**"

If Person 2 understood what Person 1 was setting up, everyone says, "Ah yes! I remember it well!"

Here's another example with that same first line:

I sat on a chair
You stood on the **floor**
I worked as a *prostitute.*
You worked as a **whore.**
Ah yes, I remember it well!

Or...

I sat on a chair
You sat on a **couch**
I stand up really *straight*
No, you really **slouch.**
Ah yes, I remember it well!

So the prostitute setup isn't an opposite, but it definitely is closely associated with "whore." And the "sat on a couch" isn't totally an opposite of "sat on a chair" but it's a correction of how the first person is remembering/thinking.

The third line is very important. To be able to clearly and concisely set up a rhyme is a great skill. When I teach this in class, there are always a couple people who have a difficult time setting up another person. They want to LEAD their partners to say the word rather than making a clear statement and trusting that the partners will get it. And it rarely works unless the partner can read minds. This is a typical confusing setup:

> P1: I sat on a chair
> P2: You stood on the **floor**
> P1: I knew you were a......
> P2: ????!!!!!!

In her head, Person 1 is thinking "whore," and it seems obvious to her that, "I knew you were a" is followed by "whore." But no one else knows it! Clear and concise is important!

Of course, even if you don't know where Person 1 is going, you should still finish the verse and rhyme, making as much sense as possible.

If you're doing this exercise alone, you obviously know what rhyme you're setting up, but in this case, it becomes practice setting up a rhyme clearly and quickly. The more you do this exercise, the faster you'll think of the rhyme word and the faster you'll be able to set up rhymes. VERY good skills to have!

Do Exercise 21 now.

Exercise 22 – Limericks

This is another good rhyming exercise. And great for teaching setting up rhymes, because you don't just do one setup, but a few! This exercise can be done with just one person, two, or done in a circle, with each person taking one line.

A typical Limerick goes like this:

Da DUM da da DUM da da **a**
Da DUM da da DUM da da **a**
Da DUM da da **b**
Da DUM da da **b**
Da DUM da da DUM da da **a**

Pick a topic. Whoever goes first thinks of a landing word in that topic and ends the first line with a rhyme of that word. The next person tries to guess the word that the first person is setting up, BUT DOESN'T SAY IT! Everybody wants the last line to have the landing word, so the second person also sets up that word with a rhyme. The third person hopefully has guessed the landing word, thinks of an associated word with that word, setting it up for the fourth person to say. Finally, the fifth person takes it home, landing on that important word.

For example, say the topic is "politics." The first person may think, "Obama." But of course he doesn't say it, he sets it up...

"There once was a man of no **drama.**"

The second person thinks, "Ah! The topic is politics... he's going for Obama! I will not say it, because it's not the best time! I'm such a team player and a wonderful person, that I'll set it up so the fifth person can get the glory!"

"Who had a pet doggie and **llama.**"

The third person has also guessed that the landing word is Obama, so thinks of an associated word ("hope") and sets it up with a rhyme.

"He wasn't a **dope**,"

The fourth person knows that the third person is setting her up with an associated word of "Obama." (Because all of our hypothetical improvisers are extremely intelligent!) Fourth person thinks to herself, "What is a word that's associated with 'Obama' that rhymes with 'dope?' Ah, 'Hope!'

"And he had so much **hope**,"

The fifth person knows that the topic is politics, and that the word being set up rhymes with "drama" and "llama."

"And that person of course was **Obama**!"

It's amazing how good groups can get at this exercise. When we first started doing this in one of the *MUSICAL! the musical* runs, it was awkward and slow, and no one knew what anyone was setting up. By the end of the run, we knew each other's thought processes so well, that this was almost a no-brainer.

Beginner improvisers have such a hard time not "jumping the gun," as it were, in the second line. Whether it's because they want the laugh or recognition that they "got" it, or that they just can't help themselves for other reasons, it's important to gain discipline to set up jokes and rhymes, and then deliver the punch of the joke when it's the right time. Build the tension (set up rhymes) and release it (deliver the punch/landing word) at the best time.

Do Exercise 22 now.

Making Your Verses Funnier

Unusual/Funny phrases

I've already talked about choosing more unusual, unexpected, or funny words to end your lines on, which goes a long way to making your verses funnier. But it doesn't HAVE to be a funny word. If a very ordinary word is part of a funny concept or image, that works too! For you songwriters who don't care about the humor, using unique and interesting phrases and imagery are really important as well.

Example:

I performed at my niece's Sweet 16 party (Hi, Aubrey!) Marshall and I improvised a song for her after a short interview. She's on the rowing team, and it seems she really liked being a jerk to her coach. So part of my verse was:

> You would think winning the race would be her every **day goal**
> But no, it's treating her coach like a number one **A-hole.**

Now to me, "A-hole" is a funny and unexpected word. (Premise: the word "A-hole" is funnier than the word "Asshole." Please debate.) But if I couldn't think of a funny word, I could've come up with a funny concept or image, like…

> When the coach treats Aubrey like his own dear **daughter**
> She responds by pushing his butt into the **water**.

"Water" is certainly not a funny or unusual word, especially when you're singing about rowing. But "pushing his butt into the water" is a funnier way of saying "pushing him into the water."

Jokes

To take this a step further, instead of thinking of a funny word or phrase and setting it up, you can think of a joke and set it up.

Most improvisers are familiar with the game called "185" (also known as "1001", and various other numbers). As a reminder, it's a joke-telling improv game. You get a topic or object or occupation from the audience and come up with a joke in the following structure:

> 185 _____s (whatever the audience suggested) walk into a bar.
> The bartender says, "We don't serve _____s here."
> The _____s say, "[PUNCHLINE]"

The punchline is often a pun on the suggestion. For example:

> 185 Lawyers walk into a bar.
> The bartender says, "We don't serve lawyers here – you hang around all day."
> The lawyers say, "We'll be brief."

Get it?! Get it?! A legal brief. We'll be brief......eh...um...okay, well, 185 usually doesn't get big laughs – it elicits groans. But it's EXCELLENT practice for getting in the joke mindset.

> 185 Proctologists walk into a bar.
> Bartender says, "We don't serve proctologists here."
> So the proctologists all gave him the finger!!

Yay!!

"Being brief" and "gave him the finger" are the punchlines. So in a song, we would simply set them up. (You always want to land a good punch!)

> When I go into a lawyer's office I shake like a leaf
> Billing for hours – they misname it "brief."

> In a proctologist's office, you never should linger
> Get out of there fast, or they'll give you the finger!

Exercise 23A - 185

Let's take this step-by-step. Here's a list of suggestions so you can do this exercise many times.

<u>185 suggestions</u>

lawyers

proctologists

teachers

bananas

cars

cell phones

dogs

cats

politicians

computers

toilets

Pick a suggestion and do as many 185s as you can for that topic. For example, I pick "cars." One of my 185s might be:

> 185 cars drive into a bar.
> The bartender says, "We don't serve cars here."
> The cars say, "That's okay. Anyway, we're too tired!"

Do Exercise 23A now.

Exercise 23B – 185 in Couplet Form

Put these 185 jokes into couplets. To make it easier, do it in this format:

> _____s in a bar, blah blahblahblahblah (*setup rhyme*)
> Blah blahblahblah (*more setting up the punchline*) Punchline/Joke

My joke ends in "tired" so that's what I want to rhyme. I think of a rhyme and end the first line with that.

> Cars in a bar, they want to get wired
> But when they start drinking, they find that they're too tired!

Okay, not a brilliant joke, but hey. This exercise is to get you into joke-mode, and to practice setting up the joke.

Do Exercise 23B now.

Exercise 23C – 185 Sung in Couplets

Play Track 8 and sing the couplets that you just made up. Please try to remember to have a melody as you sing. At first, your lyrics will be awkward, and might be stuffed into the beats. As you practice, you'll get faster, more eloquent and concise.

Do Exercise 23C now.

Exercise 24 – Sung Jokes in Verses

Once you get the hang of this, you can drop the "Blanks in a bar" setup and just sing any old lines. The musical game "Hoedown" (see next chapter) is a perfect example of jokey lyrics in a verse. Move on to Tracks 11-15 to sing full verses, and Tracks 18-22 to sing two verses in a row on any of the 185 suggestions or any topic you choose.

Play TRACKS 11-15 and 18-22 and do Exercise 24 now.

If you've ever listened to our Zenprov podcast, you'll know that Marshall Stern and I are all about getting out of the head and being very organic. Setting up rhymes/jokes is VERY brain-oriented, and SEEMS to contradict the easy going, "don't-think-so-hard" type of improv Marshall and I recommend and teach. It doesn't.

If you were to just practice this once or twice and then went into performance, you would absolutely be in your head, trying to remember everything. The purpose of practice is to learn a skill so well that it starts becoming automatic. It's like an athlete practicing moves over and over until the memory is in the muscles themselves. The athlete can then get out of the way during a competition, and get in the "zone" where everything comes naturally.

The same thing goes with improv. If you really study genres, you don't have to think when "film noir" or "Shakespeare" is called out. You know it. Your body knows it. It comes naturally. If you want to do something well on stage, you have to practice, practice, practice. I can't improvise rap. Well, I can, but pretty damn poorly. That's because I don't practice it. Though I can rhyme well, I just haven't practiced the rhythm, attitude, and basic style that make up good rap. If I did, I could get really good, let me tell you!

So practicing setting up your rhymes, practicing joke telling (if you want to do funny songs), practicing wonderful melodies all help you to get to the point where you can just... sing. Sing wonderful improvised songs.

♪ ♪ ♪

Chapter 7
Musical Games 201

These musical improv games are more advanced than the ones we've already discussed, mainly because each improviser usually sings an entire verse, rather than just one line. That means setting up rhymes!

Selling the style and the song is more important in these games than in the musical line games we discussed in Part 1. (Even though the Irish Drinking song has a definite style, many groups sing it with an inconsistent attitude and Irish accent…) Stage picture and personal physicality during these songs really can enhance the style.

Hoedown

Hoedown doesn't require too much musical talent! It's pretty obvious where the lines start and end, and it's a very simple **aabb** rhyme scheme. It was a favorite musical game on the show "Whose Line Is It Anyway?" (American version.) You can see lots of videos of Hoedown being performed if you go to YouTube.com and search "Whose Line Hoedown."

Pick a topic from the Topic Appendix D, play TRACK 23 and sing Hoedown verses now.

The Blues

Start slow. There are different styles and ways you can sing the Blues. Some are fast, and some are slow. I recommend that your troupe do a slower one if you are relatively new to musical improv games, since this gives you a little more time to come up with the rhymes. But please be aware of the tempo - there's nothing more tortuous than a really slow song, with umpteen verses!

Once you get better and faster at rhyming, you may want to speed up your Blues – at least have a higher energy Blues in your tool box.

Sell it! It's fine when someone sings a verse while just standing there, but it's memorable and entertaining when someone "performs" the song, really feeling the music and embodying the emotion. You got the blues! Show it! It's way more fun to watch and to perform. (It gives the audience something else to concentrate on other than just the lyrics...)

Stage picture. Consider the stage picture whenever you're rehearsing or performing. Think of five improvisers just lined up in a row, each singing their verse in order. Then think of five improvisers, really showing an attitude, scattered around the stage. As cool, bluesy music plays, one relaxed performer leans against the wall, another sits, oh-so-laid-back, straddling a backwards chair, another one stands with a foot up on another chair. It's WAY more interesting to look at, and gives a much clearer sense of the attitude and style.

It's full body improv instead of just head improv.

The standard 12-bar blues is three lines. Each line rhymes. Sometimes the first two lines are exactly the same, and then the third line rhymes. If you cannot think of a second rhyme with your landing word, then this is always an option. But I think it's more fun to have three separate rhyming lines.

When you get the suggestion for the topic of your Blues (you can ask, "What makes you really sad?" or "What make you happy?" or "What did you always want to be when you grew up?" etc...), come up with your funny word/concept, and – just like we've been practicing – SAVE that landing word for the end!

When learning the Blues, the hardest part for people to get is hearing where the three lines start and end. A lot of times, they will sing a line, and then start the next line too soon. Think of each line as 16 beats long. (You can definitely think of it as 8 beats, as we are used to doing, but I've seen most students naturally tap out 16 beats when listening.) A person typically sings for the first 9 beats, putting that rhyme word on the 9th beat. THEN YOU MUST PAUSE FOR THE NEXT 7 BEATS until the next line starts. Otherwise, it turns into a hot mess.

Listen to BB King sing "Everyday I Have the Blues." Or Muddy Waters singing "Whiskey Blues." Or James Taylor singing "Steamroller Blues." (Not the live versions, because he tends to fill in the rests in the live recordings!) Those are standard 12-bar blues, and that's how it's typically sung in the improv game!

As we've said before, rests (pauses) in music are fabulous for many reasons. Without rests, the lyrics/music would be nonstop and become annoying. It also gives your brain a little time to think, which is nice. But please don't LOOK like you're thinking. When you're doing the Blues, your mind might be screaming, "Oh damn! Chocolate! The Chocolate Blues! What's funny about chocolate?! Okay, Fannie Mae...Nestle...zits...zits! That's good! What rhymes with "zits?!" Pits, bits, lits, mitts, etc., etc...." But on the outside, your body should say, nice and cool and collected, "Oh yeah, man...that's right...I got de chocolate blues..."

It's confusing to know where the lines end because you CAN also fill the entire line with what essentially seems like two shorter lines. So instead of singing until the ninth beat and then resting for the rest of the line, you can finish your setup word on beat 7, rest for beat 8, and then land on your strong word at the end of the line. For example...

> It makes me scream, it makes me moan,
> Holdin' in my hand a huge Toblerone.

You COULD do an entire verse like this, but it would be harder, since you'd have to come up with a setup rhyme and a landing word for each of the three lines. It's more common to hear this for the first line, and then two long lines that rhyme. For example,

> Line 1:   It makes me scream, it makes me moan,
>   Holdin' in my hand a huge Toblerone.
> Line 2:   But size doesn't matter, I also like the little bits.
> Line 3:   I pay for it later, with a face all covered with zits!

Much more frequently, though, the 12-Bar Blues is just sung as three long lines:

> I love eating chocolate, big hunks and little bits. - - - - - - -
> (That's right) - I love eating chocolate, Toblerone and chocolate chips. - - - - - - -
> But I don't like the effect, 'cause my face gets all covered in zits!

Please note, the second rhyme is a creative approximate rhyme ('bits" and "chips"), which I like because then the final punch word isn't as obvious.

Pick a topic from the topic list, play Track 24 and sing a Blues verse or two or three. Try different melodies. You may want to try to sing my verses on chocolate just to see how they fit to the music (Do the two short rhyming lines make sense to the music? Do the longer lines make sense? Hint: they will if you start and stop at the right times!)

Play TRACK 24 and practice singing the Blues now.

Lounge Singer

One person in your group is the lounge singer and sits, miming playing a piano. (Unless your musician is also an improviser and wants to improvise lyrics while he/she actually plays...) The Lounge Singer gets a topic and then gives a smarmy talking intro about the song (i.e. Topic – Meditation - "I'd like to play this song for you wonderful, attractive people as a special gift to you. I grew up in the jungles of Tibet, and learned so many lessons from Buddha and his good friend the Dali Lama...but the best lesson of all was to take Me-Time. To swim in Lake Me. To float, dive, and even swallow a little of Me water in order to get to know Me. And here's a song about that...")

Then the lounge singer sings one verse (or maybe more) in the style of – you guessed it – Lounge. If you want just one person to do the entire game, it can be a full song (see next chapter on creating a full, formatted song) or the entire group can get in on it by being different characters at that lounge. They will individually approach the lounge singer, comment on the previous song and say they want to share a song they know. By their character, the musician knows what style it should be in. A cowboy-ish character is probably asking for a country western style. A hippie character needs a Folk Song. A loud, upper-crust fancy person may get Opera. Whatever. It can totally fit the character, or the musician may want to have fun and do a style that is very different from the character. It's up to you. Point is, each character who wants to sing comes up and sings a verse in a particular style about the given topic.

Bartender/Advice

This game is also done on Whose Line Is It Anyway?, so you can go to YouTube and search "Whose Line Bartender" and see many examples of it. For those of you with no computer, here's how it works...

One person is the bartender. (Or the therapist, if you're doing it in psychotherapy group session.) The bartender can get the suggestions, or someone to the side can – either way, when a character cozies up to the bar, we need to get what his/her problem is. Typical "gets" are – "this person is in love with something unusual," or "this person is angry/upset/obsessed about something," or have the audience tell you everything –"this person is feeling some emotion, what is it?" (Anger) "Yes, this person is angry, but not about anything that typically makes us angry. What is she angry about?" (Lint!) You're trying to elicit a topic that this person can have a problem with. The character usually sings one verse of the problem (describing it in an amusing light), and then the bartender usually sings one verse on a funny solution to that problem.

You can sing more than one verse and even go back and forth between the character and the bartender, but watch out for it going too long. Being able to sing succinctly is a great skill to have. Although, so is having fun. Balance the two!

♪ ♪ ♪

Part 3

Musical Improv 301
(Distinguished Level)

Chapter 8
Parts of a Song

Knowing song formats is incredibly important. With these structures, your improvised songs will seem written. Your improv and written songs will have variety and be more interesting for those listening. Your improv group can create original short-form game songs. You'll be able to sing in groups. You'll live longer and healthier lives! The world will be yours!!!

My thanks to Steve Gilbane for introducing me to the concept of song formats from the book *The Songwriters Idea Book*, by Sheila Davis, and to Marshall Stern for educating me more in depth to song parts as only a professional songwriter can!

The Hook

This is the most important part of the song. It's called "the hook" because it grabs you and doesn't let go. It catches and holds your attention, and it's the part that you will be singing and whistling long after the song itself is over. (A well-designed hook is like a virus – once you catch it, you can't get rid of it and it has to run its course!)

The hook is what the song is about, all condensed into a few words and notes, and must be repeated several times during the song. So it's a musical and lyrical hook.

It tends to be highest or lowest part of the song, since it's really distinctive from the rest of the song.

It is almost always the title of the song.

Some great hooks:

How Can I Miss You if You Won't Go Away

Somewhere Over the Rainbow

Help

I Got Friends in Low Places

You Can't Always Get What You Want

Love the One You're With

Blowin' in the Wind

You Can Call Me Al

Good Vibrations

Let it Be

When songs don't use the hook as the title, we never know the real title of the song. Take The Who's song "Baba O'Reilly." Don't know it? Not surprising, since it's never even said in the song! Most people know it as "Teenage Wasteland" since that's what's repeated over and over.

Most songwriters write around a good hook. Why? If you have a good hook and the rest of the song sucks, the people will remember the hook and think it's a great song. (I say the same thing about ending strongly – if you have a strong ending, people will forget the suckiness that came early on!)

Verse

The verse is the basic building block of a song. It's where the story is told, where we learn the character's situation and/or mental state. It's what moves the story along – the flesh of the story, if you will. For you musicians, musically it usually starts on the tonic, or the I (1). Energetically, it's the lowest of the song (because we're getting the back story, the information, etc., here, which might not be THAT exciting), but it drives the song to the hook.

Marshall says it's called a verse because it's versatile and always changing. That "verse" comes from "versatile." I asked him if that was true, and he admitted he didn't know, but that it sounded good!

Each verse is musically the same, so you try to keep the same melody, length of lines and meter.

When I talk about a verse, I'll abbreviate it as "V," and follow Sheila Davis' lead and use a square:

Chorus

When you have a chorus in a song, it will always contain the hook (the title!) In fact, the chorus is one big hook - it's catchy and stays in your brain. I've heard that it comes from olden days, in public drinking places, so people could easily sing along when a song started up. (Drinking alcohol made it even harder to remember things, so choruses had to be memorable!) It was also used in the Civil War, to get soldiers and citizens all hopped up for their side.

The energy really rises in the chorus. Musically it is different from the verse, usually going up to the IV or the VI. The melody should be totally different than the verse melody.

A chorus is usually two, four or six lines. I'm going to have you sing four line choruses, just to keep things consistent. But your musician may prefer another length, so get on the same page with him/her, if you're improvising. Get on the same page with yourself, if you're composing songs.

Here are some key points about choruses:

1. The chorus should be **simple**.

   ✕ Remember, choruses were for people to join the song and sing along. If the words and music were really complicated, it wouldn't work.

   ✕ Often, the title is repeated more than once during the chorus, so that helps it to stay simple.

   ✕ The chorus MUST be simple if you're improvising, so you can actually REMEMBER it when it comes back. I don't know how many times I've been in a class or a show when someone tries to get all clever during a chorus, and the lines get really complicated. When it's time to sing the chorus again, it's not just the other improvisers who can't remember it, but the person who *created* the chorus can't!

2. The chorus must **repeat**.

   ✕ If it doesn't, it's not a chorus!

3. The chorus must **contrast** with the rest of the song.

   ✕ Many inexperienced accompanists just play the same musical chords for the chorus as they do with the verse. Sometimes they go to a different key, but the style and rhythm are exactly the same. NO GOOD. It really needs to contrast, not only for pleasing variety, but so the improvisers know beyond a shadow of a doubt that, yes, THIS is the chorus. It should be clear we have left the verse and gone to the chorus. So the musician plays something different, and the singer SINGS something different, too! Sing a different melody! (Remember, if you always improvise/sing in one-note melodies, the verse will sound just like the chorus, and this is VERY unsatisfying!)

4. A chorus can **stand on its own** – it's like a mini song.

   × If you played the chorus without the rest of the song, it would seem complete.

5. A chorus should be the **highest energy** and **most interesting** and **memorable** part of the song. As we said in the hook section, usually the title/hook is the highest or lowest part of the song, making it contrast the most and stand out.

6. A chorus must **arrive quickly.**

   × Remember, the chorus is the highest energy and most interesting and memorable part of the song. Don't make people wait too long to hear it! If the verse before rambles on, we'll lose interest. This may be okay if your audience is trapped in the theater and can't leave, but really, do you WANT to torture them?!

A chorus will be abbreviated "C" and shown as a circle.

Bridge

A bridge also ups the energy of a song. It's a break from the predictability of the song.

1. The chord progression is different from the verse (and chorus) and has a totally different melody from the verse (and chorus.)

2. Often, the bridge brings in some new information.

3. Because it's an auditory break from the rest of the song, not only is the melody different, but the rhyme scheme can be as well.

4. Usually the bridge does NOT have the title in it.

5. A bridge is often two or four lines. Michael Pollock, one of my fabulous contributing musicians for this book, likes to do eight-line bridges! Just for rhyming practice and consistency, I'll have you do four-line bridges, but your musician will probably have an inclination to a certain number of lines for his/her bridges. It's a good idea to know what s/he tends to do. That's why you practice – to get on the same page.

A bridge will be abbreviated "B" and shown as a triangle:

♪ ♪ ♪

Chapter 9
Song Formats

Verse Songs - The most basic song format

Many improv song games are this simplest of structures. It's verse, verse, verse, etc. It can be as many verses as you want, but please don't go on and on just because you can – think of your listener!

Each verse is musically just like the last. The melody is usually the same. Musicians call this an AAA song format. I stay away from using this name, just so you don't mix it up with an **aaa** rhyme scheme! In fact, I'll call it a Verse song (or VVV), since the only thing in it are verses!

Think of the typical improvised blues. Or of the hoedown on the TV show "Whose Line Is It, Anyway?" The musician plays the same verse/chord progression every time, and the improvisers merely take their turn singing the entire verse, lyrics inspired by the topic given by the audience. The music is the same for each verse, but the lyrics are different.

In written Verse songs, the title is usually in the same place in each verse. But in MOST improvised Verse song games, each verse is usually just four lines about the topic, with no title.

Verse songs CAN be boring, but they certainly don't have to be. This format is perfect for telling stories. Its simplicity is also great for children's rhymes/songs. Since it IS the same musical progression and melody each verse, there are things you can do to spice it up:

1. Add instruments/voices each verse. The first verse can start very simply, with few instruments (if you're writing a song) or with one singer (if you're improvising on stage.) Then, as each verse comes in, add a new instrument/voice. This builds the energy of the song so it feels like there's actually something happening, rather than just the same old thing repeating.

2. Do a key change/modulation toward the end of the song between verses. This is a huge energy booster! I have a friend (Hi, Adam Felber!) who had a band in college. They played a polka version of "Purple Rain," and modulated EVERY verse! By the end, it was in an incredibly high key. Very funny.

3. Keep the title and other ideas consistent in the song, so the listener feels grounded (see examples below). I suppose the most simple and obvious example of this would be "99 Bottles of Beer on the Wall." It certainly is the same musical verse every time – in fact, the only word that changes each verse is the number. But the concept, that a bottle gets taken and passed around so that there's one less on the wall, so the number is going to decrease by one every time, is always there. This actually sets up some tension as you anticipate the lower and lower number in each verse!

Here are some well-known (well, some of them) examples of Verse Songs:

Mary Had a Little Lamb

Do Your Ears Hang Low?

On Top of Spaghetti

Kumbaya

Amazing Grace

The Wreck of the Edmund Fitzgerald (Gordon Lightfoot)

Maggie May (Rod Stewart)

Gentle On My Mind (Glen Campbell)

Let's analyze a couple of Verse song examples, and see how they're put together and work. How about starting with the classic, and oh, so socially significant, **"Do Your Ears Hang Low?"**

<u>Do Your Ears Hang Low?</u>
Do your ears hang low?
Do they wobble to and fro?
Can you tie them in a knot?
Can you tie them in a bow?
Can you throw them o'er your shoulder
Like a Continental Soldier?
Do your ears hang low?

Do your ears hang high?
Do they reach up to the sky?
Do they wrinkle when they're wet?
Do they straighten when they're dry?
Can you wave them at your neighbor
With an element of flavor?
Do your ears hang high?

> **Do your ears hang wide?**
> Do they flap from side to side?
> Do they wave in the breeze
> From the slightest little sneeze?
> Can you soar above the nation
> With a feeling of elevation?
> **Do your ears hang wide?**
>
> **Do your ears fall off**
> When you give a great big cough?
> Do they lie there on the ground
> Or bounce up at every sound?
> Can you stick them in your pocket
> Just like Davy Crocket?
> **Do your ears fall off?**

"**Do Your Ears Hang Low?**" is not a story song, but one searching for answers. Namely, the answer of how your ears hang.

So each verse poses a question at the beginning of how your ears might hang, and then gives descriptions of how they might look/ behave when they hang that way. (Consistency)

The first and last line of each verse is the same. (Consistency)

The rhyme scheme DOES change, oddly enough. It goes from **aabacca** in the first two verses, to **aabbcca** in the second two. (Not consistent, but close enough – it doesn't make a huge difference to our ears (!) as we listen to it. Although maybe the composer wanted our ears to fall off, so we could experience the song in a deep and meaningful manner. Wow. I never knew this was such an intense song!

It helps some people to think of each verse as four regular lines, with INTERNAL rhymes in most lines, instead of thinking of it as eight short lines. Then it would be:

First two Verses: aa

                        a

                       bb

                        a

Second two Verses: aa

                        bb

                        cc

                        a

Here's one song called "The Ballad of the Shape of Things," (Written by Sheldon Harnick, performed by Kingston Trio and countless others!) which I learned for a cabaret show. It just demonstrates good lyric writing – think of these things if you're composing written songs and even when you're improvising…

The Ballad of the Shape of Things

Completely round is the perfect pearl
The oyster manufactures;
Completely round is the steering wheel
That leads to compound fractures.
Completely round is the golden fruit
That hangs from the orange tree.
Yes, the circle shape is quite renowned,
And sad to say, it can be found
In the low down, dirty runaround
My true love gave to me, yes,
My true love gave to me.

Completely square is the velvet box
He said my ring would be in.
Completely square is the envelope
He said farewell to me in.
Completely square is the handkerchief
I flourish constantly,
As I dry my eyes of the tears I shed,
And blow my nose that turned bright red;
Completely square is my true love's head:
He will not marry me, no, he will not marry me.

Rectangular is the hotel door
My true love tried to sneak through.
Rectangular is the transom
Over which I had to peek through.
Rectangular is the hotel room I entered angrily.
And rectangular is the wooden box,
Where lies my love 'neath the golden phlox.
They say he died from the chicken pox,
In part I must agree: one chick too many had he!

Triangular is the piece of pie
I eat to ease my sorrow.
Triangular is the hatchet blade
I plan to hide tomorrow.
Triangular the relationship
That now has ceased to be.
And triangular is the garment thin
That fastens on with a safety pin
To a prize I had no wish to win;
It's a lasting memory that my true love gave to me.

- Sheldon Harnick, "Ballad of the Shape of Things," 1956

The title doesn't even appear in the song, but it summarizes what the song is about, so I don't mind!

Good things about this song that you should think about using:

1. Consistent thematic device – shapes, or, more specifically, comparing a shape to what's going on in the singer's relationship.

2. Irony – "my true love."

3. Interesting Descriptions – rather than just flat out telling. ("garment thin that fastens on with a safety pin" rather than just saying "diaper," or "wooden box" rather than just saying "coffin.")

4. Alliteration – "perfect pearl," "low down dirty," "piece of pie." Alliteration is really fun to hear.

5. Fun Rhyme Scheme and Meter – I love the three shorter lines towards the ends of each verse that rhyme and either set up or end in a joke. ("And rectangular is the wooden box where lies my love 'neath the golden phlox. They say he died from the chicken pox, In part I must agree: one chick too many had he!") I know we tend to just do four lines of **aabb** rhyming, but as you get better, and you get more familiar with your musician, try branching out to extra lines and interesting rhyme schemes.

Another great Verse song is Jimmy Webb's "By the Time I Get to Phoenix," It tells a story. Every verse starts with the idea of "by the time I get to [location], my wife will be doing X," which gives us a very dynamic story line. We simultaneously see the guy traveling east, and his woman slowly realizing that he's gone. It's like we get to peek into this private and life-changing day in the lives of these characters.

Okay. We've seen that the Verse song is a good format for improv games, story songs, children's and folk songs, and although the form is simple, it doesn't have to be a very simple song.

Exercise 25 – Individual Verses

One verse at a time. If you've been practicing the improv games from Chapter 2, then you've been practicing Verse songs, although they were verses with the topic as the only cohesive part.

For this exercise, play Tracks 11-15 and use a title from the title appendix as the first line. That's it – one verse, the title goes in the first line. So if you're doing an **aabb** rhyme scheme, then it's: title (a), rhyming to the title line (a), setup rhyme line (b), associated landing word/phrase line (b).

If I picked the title, oh, say… "Lounging in Bed," MY thought process is as follows…

1. I know I have to rhyme "bed" so I make sure I have a rhyme for that. Hmmm, tons of rhymes…head, dead, said…I know any of those can work, so I stop there and choose one.

2. I choose "head," because I connect it a bit in MY head with lounging in bed.

3. Think of a funny (if you're going for comedy) or associated word/phrase.

4. I think… "slob."

5. Now think of a rhyme for "slob" – Bob, sob, knob, job.

6. Choose one.

So perhaps my improv verse comes out as…

> Lounging in Bed,
> Nothing in my head
> But thoughts of my job.
> Thank God I'm a professional Slob.

Play TRACKS 11-15 and do Exercise 25 now.

Very good. Once you get solid in doing one verse, go on to the next exercise!

༄ ༄ ༄ ༄ ༄ ༄

Please Note – In a live class, a title is picked, and the musician usually plays something that really embodies the feel of that title. Since these are prerecorded accompaniments, you might get lovely, melodic music with a really mean spirited title. That's okay. It's a form of musical irony, and you can use the sweet to really showcase how mean you actually are. If you get a title and music that are opposing each other, try different things. Sing the sweet song sweetly with sweet lyrics except for the title. Sing the sweet song sweetly with mean lyrics, sing the sweet song nastily with sweet lyrics. Sing the sweet song nastily with mean lyrics. See how they give different impressions of the character who is singing. Discover what works best for you.

༄ ༄ ༄ ༄ ༄ ༄

Exercise 26 – Verses in a Row

Now you'll try two verses in a row, using a consistent title or strong lyrical theme. (Like "Do Your Ears Hang (fill in the blank)" or "By the time I get to (fill in the blank)")

Play Tracks 18-22 which have two verses in a row. Choose a title from the list, or make up your own title – it will be the first line in each verse.

Randomly pick a number from 1-20 and look up the corresponding song title from Appendix E. You'll notice that one word in the title is italicized/bold. You can sing the title exactly as written (as the first line in both verses in this exercise) or you can replace this word every verse with a different word, thus making it a running theme. (Like "Do Your Ears Hang ___" is the first line of every verse with "Do Your Ears Hang Low," "Do Your Ears Hang High," "Do Your Ears Hang Wide," etc.)

And just for practice on endings, notice that some of the second verses have a big ending, as if this is the last verse of the song. (Track 19 by Spitznagel is really good for this.) You want a strong, big ending! Don't fizzle out. Repeat your last line, or the title of the song. Sell it!!!

Play TRACKS 18-22 and do Exercise 26 now.

If you can do this format, it's a small step to the next format, which is just so wonderful!

Tagline

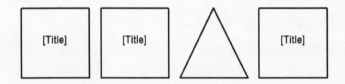

I love the Tagline song format! It is so elegant and classic, and can be very dramatic! When anyone improvises an entire song by themselves on stage, a Tagline song is soooo impressive to the audience. It seems like a real, written song.

Musicians call this format AABA, which can also stand for an **aaba** rhyme scheme, or the Asian American Bar Association, or the All-American Basketball Alliance, or Alpha-Aminobutyric acid, an isomer of the amino acid aminobutyric acid. That's too confusing, so I just call it a Tagline song!

You don't hear many contemporary songs written in the Tagline format – it was very popular in the first half of the 20th century. It still can be heard in country, gospel, jazz and theater, but not as often as it used to be. One of the reasons these songs seem so classic is that Cole Porter, Ira and George Gershwin, and all those great composers mainly used this song format.

Verses in a Tagline Song

1. In a Tagline Song, the title (or Tagline) is found in the same place in every verse. It will either be in the first line of each verse (First Line Tagline), in the last line of each verse (Last Line Tagline), or sometimes it's in the first AND last line of each verse.

2. Each verse is musically the same. The lyrics will be different, of course, but the chord progression and melody should be the same for every verse in a song. (Or as similar as you can make them if you're improvising!)

The Bridge

1. Shows up to keep things from getting too monotonous.

2. It is musically very different from the verses. It MUST contrast with the verses.

3. It can have a different rhyme scheme.

4. It can be a different length. (A verse typically has four lines, but a bridge can have two to eight lines.)

5. Lyrically, don't put the title in the bridge (It's supposed to be a break – you want to get away from "Verse-y" qualities.)

6. There will often be new information that comes out in the bridge, so that when the title comes back, it will mean something a little different. (i.e. Verse 1 – "I Miss You," Verse 2 – "I Miss You," Bridge – "I Killed You!" Ah, so when "I Miss you" comes back in Verse 3, it now means something more!)

7. This is a good time to explore different ways the character feels about what he/she is singing about. (i.e. Verses are about "I want to marry you," then bridge can be "But then I'll lose my freedom," "I'll be trapped," etc. etc.)

The Ending

1. The ending of any song is hugely important! It can save an otherwise stinky song. Since it's the last thing people hear, they will tend to forget the earlier mediocrity and downright putrid-ness that might have come before, IF the song ends very strongly and confidently.

2. Use a tag or a button by repeating the last line one or more times, or summing the song up with a spoken line (sums up verbally) or a sung melody with no words or a sound effect (sums up emotionally.)

3. There are infinite ways to end, but your song should always sound like it is absolutely ending with purpose. There's nothing worse than a song petering out to nothing. The audience rarely claps when a song peters out. With a good, strong ending, the audience will go wild because you give them an obvious button. Which would you rather have?

Examples

Let's look at a well-known first line Tagline song...

> **Over the Rainbow**
> VERSE 1: **Somewhere over the rainbow**
> Way up high,
> There's a land that I heard of
> Once in a lullaby

VERSE 2: **Somewhere over the rainbow**
>   Skies are blue,
>   And the dreams that you dare to dream
>   Really do come true.

BRIDGE: Someday I'll wish upon a star
>   And wake up where the clouds are far behind me.
>   Where troubles melt like lemon drops
>   Away above the chimney tops
>   That's where you'll find me.

VERSE 3: **Somewhere over the rainbow**
>   Bluebirds fly.
>   Birds fly over the rainbow.
>   Why then, oh why can't I?

EXTRA ENDY THINGY:
>   If happy little bluebirds fly
>   Beyond the rainbow
>   Why, oh why can't I?
>   *- Arlen and Harburg, "Over the Rainbow," 1939*

You'll notice that each verse starts with the title (first line Tagline.) And the bridge sounds completely different, going to a new place, musically and lyrically. After Verse 3 there is a little extra combination of the verse and bridge that ritards (slows down) for the ending (a coda, or for you songwriters - an extended tag.)

Is there new information introduced in the bridge? Not shocking news, but it does introduce a new element. I would say Information-wise, the song goes:

>   V1: There's a great place
>   V2: There's a great place
>   B: Someday I'M going to be there
>   V3: There's a great place, and why can't I be there?

So the new information in the bridge DOES change the third verse.

Here's another one, this time a last line Tagline song...

> **Peace**
> VERSE 1:Boiling black clouds roiling in from the west
> Clashing claps of thunder sent to steal my rest
> Won't they ever cease? Won't I ever find
> **Peace**
>
> VERSE 2:Like gently rolling swaying swells out at sea
> Just the moon the stars the waves and me
> I've been on my knees, I'd give anything to find
> **Peace**
>
> BRIDGE:Peace come take me home
> Make me one of your own
> Purge me 'til the only thing I feel
> Is **Peace**
>
> VERSE 3:I've had moments sitting staring into space
> With a calm and placid look on my face
> God I treasure these precious moments of
> **Peace**
> Sweet **Peace**
> *- Marshall Stern, "Peace," 1994*

Even though the title is just one word, it is the entire last line of every verse. In Tagline songs, sometimes the title is the entire line, sometimes it's just part of the line. But it's always there! I love the lyric quality of this song – there is alliteration, internal rhymes, similes, etc. (All of which we'll cover in Part 4 of Instant Songwriting, including the "etc."!) The title does show up in the bridge, which is a bit unusual, but since the title is only one word, it doesn't stand out too much.

And did you notice the interesting rhyme scheme? If you look quickly, you may think it's **aabc**, but in the middle of the the third line there is always a rhyme with the Tagline ("cease" "knees" and "these" with "Peace.")

Here are some other great examples of Tagline songs:

Someone To Watch Over Me (George and Ira Gershwin)

Bewitched, Bothered and Bewildered (Rodgers and Hart)

The Lady is a Tramp (Rodgers and Hart)

Great Balls of Fire (Jerry Lee Lewis)

Blue Moon (Rodgers and Hart)

Will You Still Love Me Tomorrow (The Shirelles)

Verse Verse Bridge Verse (VVBV) is the most basic format of the Tagline songs, but you DO see VVBVBV formats, where the songwriter adds another bridge and final verse. The Beatles use this format a lot (i.e. "I'll Follow the Sun," "Hey Jude," "I Want to Hold Your Hand.") You can even find VVBVBVBV songs out there! But the point is that you should be familiar with and able to improvise/compose in the basic VVBV format before exploring and screwing around with it.

Exercise 27 – Last Line Tagline Verses

You've already been practicing doing verses with a first line Tagline (title) in the Verse Songs section. Now let's practice doing verses with last line Taglines. I've been musically improvising for many, many years, and I tell you, the audience goes nuts for last line Tagline songs. When you set up the tagline and it comes back, there is something sooooo satisfying and pleasing to the ear and emotions.

We'll start with just one verse. Pick a title from Appendix E, and then play a one-verse track (11-15). Sing the four lines of your verse. You only really have to worry about three lines, because you already know the fourth line. It's the title you picked out.

Exercise 27A - abcb Rhyme Scheme

Let's start simply and do an **abcb** rhyme scheme. That way, you only have to worry about one rhyme – the rhyme with your title.

For example, say I picked the title, "My Broken Lace." I know "My Broken Lace" is my fourth line, and I need one rhyme for Lace. I pick "face," and the phrase "tears on my face" just comes to me, since "My Broken Lace" makes me feel sad. So already I have most of my verse…

_____

Tears on my face.

_____

My Broken Lace.

Since I know I don't have to rhyme the other lines, I can fill it in with anything which speaks to my sadness or tragedy (as I'm feeling it) of my broken lace. Maybe it's…

Desolation, loneliness,
Tears on my face.
My life is ripped asunder -
My Broken Lace.

So pick a title, and sing an abcb rhyme scheme, setting up your last line title with a rhyme in the second line.

Play a TRACK from 11-15 and do Exercise 27A now.

Exercise 27B – abab Rhyme Scheme

Pick another title and track, but this time try an abab rhyme scheme. It's like the one you just did, but this time your first and third line will rhyme with each other.

Play a TRACK from 11-15 and do Exercise 27B now.

Exercise 27C - aabb Rhyme Scheme

Pick another title and track, but do an **aabb** rhyme scheme, where your third line will set up the fourth line title.

Play a TRACK from 11-15 and do Exercise 27C now.

Note: Rhyme schemes are very useful things in a song. As mentioned before, it's more than just knowing when to rhyme and when not to. Rhymes actually help set up tension in a song. Tension is very important in any artistic endeavor. We should understand tension in our regular improv scenes as well as in our songs. (What's worse than setting up tension in a scene, and then someone enters and breaks the tension before it's time? Well, maybe having no tension whatsoever, which makes for very boring scenes...) When you set up a rhyme, there is tension until you rhyme it. Rhyming resolves the tension. So the **abab** rhyme scheme delivers more tension than an **aabb**, since the listener must wait longer to get the rhyme. (You don't want them to wait too long, or they'll forget and it's like having no tension at all.) An **aaab** rhyme scheme has a different feel, but still builds the tension, since there are three rhymes in a row, the listener expects a fourth, but it is resolved with the tagline. Improvisers tend to do straight **aabb** rhyme schemes since it's easier to remember words, but I recommend really mixing your rhyme schemes up!

Exercise 27D – aaab Rhyme Scheme

Do it again, but now do an **aaab** rhyme scheme, like the song "Lady is a Tramp" and "Bewitched, Bothered and Bewildered," both by Rodgers and Hart.

Play a TRACK from 11-15 and do Exercise 27D now.

Great. Now that you're solid with creating a verse and setting up a title, let's move onto being able to do TWO verses. Ooh, this is getting good!

Exercise 28 – Two Verses of Tagline

Pick a title and play a two-verse track (Tracks 18-22). You'll simply sing two verses, each verse ending with the title you picked. Although your words will be different for each verse (except the fourth line, which will be exactly the same – since it's the title), your rhyme scheme and melody should be the same for each verse.

Things to remember - it's tempting to sing on one note so you don't forget the melody, but that is typical bad songwriting/ improvising. You want your song to be good, and not sound like every other typical improv/written song - so have a melody!

We're also going to start working on endings. Even though you'd only really be half-way through the song after the second Tagline Verse, we're going to pretend that it's the end of the song. For this exercise, when you've finished your second verse, which MUST be when that title is sung a second time (remember, the fourth line of each verse is the title...) then I want you to end the song by singing that title again. In fact, sing it as many times as the music will allow.

Normally, you have a musician interacting and playing with you live. We just have recorded music, so do your best to end with the music so that it sounds like you're working together.

Track 19 (by Frank Spitznagel) is the best track for practicing endings in the two verses group. When you sing to this track, experiment with your endings. Repeat the title. Stretch it out. Repeat it softly. Repeat it loudly! Sing it really low or high (always a Broadway favorite ending!)

Experiment with your rhyme schemes. (But keep them the same within the same song.)

Play TRACKS 18-22 and do Exercise 28 now.

Exercise 29 – Full Tagline Song

Now that you can do two Tagline verses, let's simply add a bridge and a verse, and you can sing a complete, wonderful, impressive song all by yourself!

Pick out a title from Appendix E or just make up one of your own (BEFORE you start singing!), and then play one of the full Tagline song tracks (25-29). Let's keep the songs all last line Taglines (title is the fourth line of each verse) for now.

We'll keep the bridges to four lines, just so you can hear the same length sections. But remember, when you're improvising with a musician, he or she may prefer a two-line bridge. You should be able to hear when the bridge ends and the third verse starts.

Remember that the bridge should contrast with the verses, so you want a totally different melody, and you can switch up rhyme schemes and rhythms if you want.

And also remember to end the song strongly. We should be able to say, "By gosh and by golly! THAT was a great ending!" after we hear your song.

Play TRACKS 25-29 and do Exercise 29 now.

Repeat this exercise often. Try changing up the rhyme schemes. Change up to first line Taglines. If one song is really wordy, try another with fewer words but a nice, flowing melody. If the title was short, and you filled in extra words for the last line, try it again using ONLY those few words in every verse's last line (or first line.)

If the song is about a problem, you can organize it like this:

> Verse 1: Explain the problem.
> Verse 2: Explore the problem more (why is it such a problem?)
> Bridge: Explore the solution.
> Verse 3: Describe what will life be like once the problem is solved.

You can also organize a Tagline song along a timeline:

> Verse 1: Long ago
> Verse 2: More recent past
> Bridge: Present
> Verse 3: Future

A timeline gives a natural through-line to a song, in addition to the through-line of the title returning every verse.

Get comfortable singing an entire Tagline song. If you can do this, you are way ahead of 99% of the musical improvisers out there!

Play TRACKS 25-29 and experiment with Exercise 29.

Verse Chorus

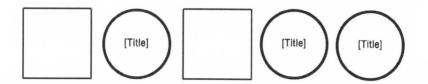

A Verse Chorus song is a ton of fun, because you can actually sing WITH other people, even though the song is being improvised! Popular music these days is almost always written in the Verse Chorus format. The format above (verse 1, chorus, verse 2, chorus, chorus) is a very basic way to put a Verse Chorus song together. You COULD have three, four, or twenty-three verses if you want! (A 23-verse song would probably be very long and boring, but hey – if you want to do that to your audience – that's up to you!) I like having two choruses at the end of an improvised song, since it usually ups the energy and gives a strong, solid ending. If the chorus is long and/or boring, it can hurt the energy of the show to repeat it yet again. The solution? Learn how to create good, strong choruses!

Since the chorus is the most important part of this kind of song, let's start there.

As we've already discussed at the beginning of this chapter, the chorus is the highest energy point in a song, and should be the most memorable. In a Verse Chorus song, the title is always in the chorus. This makes sense, since the title is the hook of the song – it's what it's all about. You want that phrase to be the most memorable, so it should get repeated.

Here is a quick review on what we already covered about Choruses:

1. The chorus must be repeated – or it's not a chorus.

2. The chorus is the highest energy and most interesting part of the song.

3. Get to the chorus quickly – since it's the best part, don't keep us waiting!

4. Contrast – the chorus must sound different than the rest of the song.

5. The chorus can stand on its own.

And most importantly…

6. KEEP THE CHORUS SIMPLE!

This is essential in musical improv, where you're going to be singing the chorus several times – if it's complicated, you won't remember it! If you have the luxury of writing the song, yes, you'll be able to read the chorus and sing it, but it should STILL be simple, so it sticks in your listeners' minds!

Here are some examples of simple choruses:

Fifteen men on the Dead Man's Chest
Yo-ho-ho, and a bottle of rum!
Drink and the devil had done for the rest
Yo-ho-ho, and a bottle of rum!
– Robert Louis Stevenson, "Dead Man's Chest," from *Treasure Island*, 1883

Too-re-loo-re-loo-ral, Too-ra-loo-ra-li,
Too-re-loo-re-loo-ral, Hush now, don't you cry!
Too-re-loo-re-loo-ral, Too-ra-loo-ra-li,
Too-re-loo-re-loo-ral, that's an Irish lullaby
- James Royce Shannon, "An Irish Lullaby," 1913

Every morning, every evening
Ain't we got fun?
Not much money, oh, but honey
Ain't we got fun?
> - Whiting, Egan and Kahn, "Ain't We Got Fun," 1921

Jingle bells, jingle bells, jingle all the way
Oh, what fun it is to ride in a one horse open sleigh
Jingle bells, jingle bells, jingle all the way
Oh, what fun it is to ride in a one horse open sleigh
> - James Lord Pierpont, "One Horse Open Sleigh," 1857

These are choruses from fairly old songs. But the concept of the simple chorus hasn't changed. More modern songs with simple choruses you may be familiar with are:

Soul Man (you know, from the movie The Blues Brothers!)
(Isaac Hayes)

We Will Rock You (Queen)

Rock & Roll All Nite (Kiss)

Pour Some Sugar on Me (Def Leppard)

Ruby (Kaiser Chiefs)

Sweet Child O' Mine (Guns 'N Roses)

Don't Cha (The Pussycat Dolls)

Rock the Casbah (The Clash)

I could go on and on and on. Notice that the titles in almost all of these examples are repeated in the chorus. If not, then at least another line is repeated verbatim, keeping the chorus simple.

A chorus is NOT a verse. Please don't have four completely different lines, like you do in a verse. At least not until you get really adept in making and remembering choruses. And even then I recommend that at LEAST two lines be lyrically the same (like in the "Dead Man's Chest" example above.)

Exercise 30A – Good Choruses

Let's practice making and remembering good choruses. Tracks 30-34 are Choruses. There will be a musical lead-in where I'll give the beat in snaps, and then it will go immediately into a chorus. We'll make them all four lines of eight beats each, just to be consistent. (Please be aware, that some of the tracks have such a fast 8 count, that they seem more like 4 beat lines. I note any unusual properties of the tracks - like a really fast beat - on the web page with the tracks.)

Your musician or group might prefer a two-line chorus, or an eight-line chorus. That's fine. Just remember that every time the chorus comes back, you try to make it exactly the same, so if the first time you sing a chorus it's eight lines, then every time you go back to it, it should be eight lines.

For this exercise, pick a title out of the Appendix E. I want you to sing these lyrics for each of the four lines. So just like "Soul Man," you'll sing the title four times, once for each line. Now, those are just the lyrics. "Soul Man" has the exact same melody for each line as well. Try singing your first line melody four times as well and see how it goes. Most of the time, it sounds awkward, especially in the last line. If the music goes to a different place, you should, too. And try to make the last line sound like the ending. This may mean you have to cheat a little to make it sound like it really fits with the ending.

For example, if you pick the title "I'm Going to the Beach Again," it might be:

I'm Going to the Beach Again
I'm Going to the Beach Again
I'm Going to the Beach Again
To the Beach Again

Really listen to that last line and don't force too many words if it doesn't fit.

Watch your melodies. Although one note for the entire chorus would be simple and easy to remember, it's very boring. Have a nice melody line – THAT'S a big part of making a memorable hook and chorus.

The tracks will play two choruses in a row. So the first chorus you're improvising, and then for the second chorus, you simply repeat exactly what you sang for the first chorus!

Play a TRACK from 30-34 and do Exercise 30A now.

How did that go? Did you remember your chorus? The lyrics shouldn't have been difficult to remember since it was all the same line, but was your melody so complicated that you couldn't remember what you sang? Was the rhythm too complicated? Was it too boring? Did the ending sound natural or forced?

If the chorus didn't sound fabulous to you, try it again. Same track, same title. Fix whatever was off. If your melody was so complicated that you couldn't remember it, then make it a little simpler. (PLEASE no one-note melodies!!!) Or if it was too simple and boring, then move around a bit more, melodically. If the ending didn't sound really natural (too many words, too few words, melody didn't fit with the music), then try again, changing it up.

Play the same TRACK 30-34 with the same title.

I hope that felt and sounded better. If not, no worries. You can practice this until you are absolutely fabulous!

Exercise 30B – Filling Various Beats

I know you want to move on. But let's just stick with that same title you've been using. I want you to experiment with it, so you can feel the different ways to sing a line. Use the same track as well.

If you filled all eight beats of the line with words last time, I want you to sing it all in four beats, and then rest for the last four beats of every line. This may mean you have to sing the words very quickly. Try it. If you filled four beats last time, fill all eight beats with the title. Then sing it again and fill five beats of the eight. Then try filling six beats of the eight.

This goes for the first three lines. For the fourth line, do whatever sounds natural to end the chorus. Try different things to see what works.

Play the same track and do Exercise 30B with the same title.

Okay. Very good. Remember this when you sing choruses. You don't have to fill in every single beat with words. And try different melodies. When improvisers sing choruses, they tend to sing very similar melody lines, and fill the same amount of beats. Some improvisers are four-beat fillers. Some are eight-beat fillers. It's nice if you know what you tend to do, and are able to break out of it so your choruses sound unique each time you sing a different song.

Another way improvisers get stuck in a rut is to sing the same rhyme/line sequence each song. What we've been practicing in the past few exercises is:

Title
Title
Title
Title

Perfectly valid, but you don't want to get stuck doing every chorus in every song like this.

Exercise 31 – Practicing Different Choruses

Exercise 31A

Play another Track from 30-34, and pick a different title. This time do:

> Title
> Title
> Title
> Different, non-rhyming line

For example, if the title is "Red Face and Rum," it might be

> Red Face and Rum
> Red Face and Rum
> Red Face and Rum
> Ah, Bahamas, my home

Or try it backwards:

> Non rhyming line
> Same non rhyming line
> Same non rhyming line
> Title
>
> Ah, Bahamas, my home
> Ah, Bahamas, my home
> Ah, Bahamas, my home
> Red Face and Rum

In the first example, you're repeating the title several times, so it stands out. In the second example, although the title is only said once, it stands out from the rest of the chorus. Either way works well for a memorable hook.

Please note: if the title you're working with is really long, you can split it up into different lines. Using this line sequence, if the title were "I Know You Said You Were Lazy, But This Takes the Cake" it could be:

I Know You Said You Were Lazy
I Know You Said You Were Lazy
I Know You Said You Were Lazy
But this takes the Cake

Play a TRACK from 30-34 and do Exercise 31A now.

Try it again, but this time use a rhyming line, rather than a non-rhyming line.

Just a beach bum
Just a beach bum
Just a beach bum
Red Face and Rum

(By the way, I'm teaching improv on a cruise right now, and my face is bright red from the sun, and I had some rum… write what you know about!)

Keep singing the same two choruses in a row for each exercise, rather than doing a short cut and doing a non-rhyming chorus followed immediately by a rhyming one. This will build the skill of remembering what exactly you sang so you can recall better in the future. If you consistently can't remember what you just sang, there's something too complicated about it (lyrics, melody, or rhythm.) Better to figure that out now, so you can correct it. You need to sing a memorable chorus so not just you, but your fellow players can sing it when it comes back.

Play a TRACK from 30-34 and try this rhyming line sequence now.

Exercise 31B

Pick a title, play a track from 30-34, and do this sequence:

>   Line (rhyming or not with title)
>   Title
>   Same line as line 1
>   Title

A non-rhyming example for the title "Seared Skin":

>   Don't forget the SPF
>   Seared Skin
>   (I said) Don't forget the SPF
>   Seared Skin

A rhyming example:

>   Burnin' is a sin.
>   Seared Skin
>   (I said) Burnin' is a sin.
>   Seared Skin

Play a TRACK from 30-34 and do Exercise 31B now.

Exercise 31C

Same deal. Try this sequence:

>   Title
>   Title
>   Non Rhyming Line
>   Title

And of course you can rhyme:

Title
Title
Rhyming Line
Title

Play TRACKS 30-34 and do Exercise 31C now.

Exercise 31D

Same drill again. Try this sequence:

Title
Non rhyming line
Different line rhyming with line 2
Title

Lightly Snoring Next to Me
Early to bed
Stuffy in the head
Lightly Snoring Next to Me

Play TRACKS 30-34 and do Exercise 31D now.

Exercise 31E

I could keep going and give you different sequences. But you can come up with them yourself, too! Keep going (or if you've had enough, go on and come back later) by thinking up a sequence and trying it out. Some things to remember...

1. You MUST have the title in the chorus.

2. One line (usually the title, but not necessarily) should repeat at least once. (So at the MOST complicated, you have three different lyric lines.)

As you work on your choruses, notice your melodies. Do they tend to be similar? This is practice, so practice doing things you don't usually do.

Notice your rhythms. Are they really on the beat? Or are they more adventurous? Try different rhythms and different lengths of your lines. (The music will always be eight beats long for each line, but that doesn't mean you have to fill those eight beats with words. Try filling different amounts of beats.)

If your chorus is difficult to remember, it may be because you're doing something really weird with the rhythm. That's cool, if it's done clearly. But if it's a haphazard, random type of rhythm, you and especially your fellow improvisers will have a tough time repeating it. Back off and do more normal rhythms until you can do those well, then slowly get more complicated. You'll hopefully learn how to do interesting rhythms while making them clear and memorable.

ᔉᔌᔉᔌᔉᔌ

You can always clap or snap or do some dance move to fill in beats/off-beats to make where you come in/start singing more memorable. For example, if you're doing an interesting rhythm of the chorus line, "Three cents a text" of, say,

Three	cents			a text			
1	2	3	4	5	6	7	8

might be hard to remember when it comes back.

Three	cents	(*clap**clap**clap*)	a text			(*clap**clap**clap*)	
1	2	3	4	5	6	7	8

makes it way more memorable and easy to duplicate.

ᔌᔉᔌᔉᔌᔉ

Notice your lyrics. They don't have to be wordy sentences. They can be poetic phrases. Or nonsense syllables. ("Yo ho ho, and a bottle of rum!") Try one or two words per line and see how that differs from many words in a line.

Play TRACKS 30-34 and do Exercise 31E now.

Pet Peeve: improvisers who start singing with the chorus after the first line. What the he...? You have no idea where the singer might want to take the chorus. He may not want to repeat the line he just sang. You're sort of forcing him to. Please be polite and let him finish the chorus, and then you can join in when it comes back! Unless you have preplanned exactly what type of chorus you will be singing, like for a short-form game, and you KNOW that it's:

Title
Title
Rhyming line,
Title

Just because people in your group tend to sing the same type of chorus, don't FORCE them to!

Exercise 32 – Entire Verse Chorus Songs

Now let's sing some full Verse Chorus Songs. We'll do a really simple Verse-Chorus-Verse-Chorus-Chorus (VCVCC) format. The verses are where you tell a story or expound on the idea of the song. The chorus is the hook, where the meaning of the song is distilled down to a few phrases (one of the phrases being the title, of course!)

Pick a title from Appendix E. That line will be in your chorus. Don't use it in your verses. So if your title is "Too Much Chocolate," Verse 1 is about chocolate or your addiction to chocolate or whatever.

You might set up rhymes for "Fannie May" or "Hershey Kiss" or "zits" or things to do with chocolate. Then the chorus will have the line "Too Much Chocolate" in it, probably more than once. If not, another line should be repeated, otherwise, it's four completely different lines, which can be hard for you to remember and not as memorable for the audience.

You'll then sing a second verse, which hopefully is close to the same melody, rhythm, and rhyme scheme of the first verse. The second verse continues Verse One's story and/or situation and/or attitude. Then sing the chorus two more times, and you're done!

Make sure to end solidly. No one likes a song that peters out and has an unsure ending. Solid. Big. Strong!

Play TRACKS 35-38 and do Exercise 32 now.

Another typical variation is to add a bridge to a Verse Chorus format. In fact, our Doo-Wop track (Track 39 by Steve Gilbane) is this format:

Songwriters out there should be aware of prechoruses (also known as a climb/lift) which is a separate section leading to the chorus.

Excellent. You can now practice and practice and get better and better at all of these formats. Try different melodies. Try different lyrics, such as lots of words versus few short staccato words versus few long drawn out words. The lyrics can be poetic or common, describing your external surroundings or your internal state. Try different rhythms. Get comfortable with all the formats, so if your musician goes into a chorus or bridge, you know that's where the song is going and aren't surprised by it. Be Master of your Musical Improv!

♪ ♪ ♪

Chapter 10
Musical Games 301

Now that you know song formats, you can create your own musical improv games, and the possibilities are endless!

Short-Form Musical Games for the Whole Troupe:

Pick a musical style, and then figure out the song format. A basic one that most improv games are is Verse Verse Verse etc. The typical improvised Blues is in this format. But at ImprovBoston, I believe we decided to sing it as:

1st person:	Verse
2nd person:	Chorus
3rd person:	Verse
4th person:	Bridge
5th person:	Verse
Everybody:	Chorus

We also decided to do an improvised Doo-Wop song. We researched that style and noticed many Doo-Wop songs were about losing something, so we decided the suggestion would be "Something that you have lost," like your keys. (Predictably, we often got "virginity" as the suggestion!) We decided in rehearsal that the song would be:

1st:	Verse 1 (Sing about Present - I'm so upset I don't have my X – what life is like without X)
2nd:	Chorus (About the item lost)
3rd:	Verse 2 (Sing about Past - we used to do X together…)
All:	Chorus
4th:	Spoken Bridge (How I lost X – doesn't have to rhyme)
5th:	Verse 3 (Future - one day I'll get you back and we'll…)
All:	Chorus
All:	Big Doo-Wop finish

Example song with "keys" as the suggestion….

Oh my keys, I'm sad as a pup,
Where did you go? My heart is locked up.
Losing you was such a sin
I can't leave the house 'cause I can't get back in.

(Chorus)
Oh Keys, My Keys, Where are you, my keys?
Oh Keys, My Keys, Where are you, my keys?
I can't replace you, I don't have the fees.
Oh Keys, Where are you, keys?

You used to jangle, and I used to sing
At the jealousy aimed at us – so many on my ring.
We laughed at people whose keys numbered three -
With you at my side, no door could stop me.

(Chorus)

(spoken Bridge) Then one day, my keys, we went to the mall.
Maybe it was at Orange Julius. Or the bathroom. Or the little
kiosk embroidering baseball caps. But when I walked outdoors,
you weren't with me. Oh, Keys - you were gone.

Someday I'll get you back, we'll never be far.
If someone tries to take you, we'll key up their car.
In the future I won't be so sloppy,
I'll take you to Home Depot and make a copy.

(Chorus)
(last line ritards to typical Doo -Wop sounding ending…)
Where – are – you – my………..(each player takes a word in descending harmony) Keys – keys – keys – keys – keys!

It seems complicated to read it, but once we practiced it a few times, it was simple for us to do. Now this is as best as I can remember how we did it. Perhaps it was a bit different, but the point is, you can put together ANY style of song, put it into a format that the whole troupe knows, and then sing that as a short-form improv game. Wheee! Your own totally unique improv song game!

Play Track 40 to hear the Doo-Wop Accompaniment.

We could have just as easily done a country and western song with the format Verse, Chorus, Verse, Chorus, Verse, Chorus, Chorus. We could've decided if the verses were about anything in particular (past, present, future or maybe the journey from friendship to love to hate with some object or person) or just random verses about whatever the suggestion was.

You can have a totally improvised chorus, or know that the title will repeat in certain lines of the chorus. For example, I used to do a fast blues when I improvised on the Disney Cruise Line. The chorus was three lines long, and the first person who sang it gave the title in the first and second line, then added a funny rhyming third rhyme, so for the suggestion "spontaneous combustion," the first chorus might be:

Oh, that really blows
Oh, that really blows
You're sittin' there and Boom! That's how it goes!

The format, with four people singing, was

Person 1:	Verse Chorus
Person 2:	Verse Chorus
Person 3:	Verse Chorus
Person 4:	Verse Chorus

So each person would sing a verse followed by the chorus. If the above was the first chorus, the second person might sing:

Oh, that really blows
Oh, that really blows
Make sure you're not wearing flammable clothes!

Of course, for the second chorus onwards, since we knew what the first two lines of the chorus would be, we could all sing together and harmonize, dropping out for the third line, so the person singing the unique line could be heard clearly. (Also subtly giving the message, "Listen to this! It's special and funny!")

The Point

The point is, once you know song formats, you can create your own special and unique musical improv game. Just pick a style, research that style to see if they tend to use a certain format or other gimmicks that you can parody, and then set the format. One person can sing the entire song, or the whole troupe can divide it and sing individual verses/choruses/bridges or even individual lines. You decide. It's that easy!

♪ ♪ ♪

Part 4

Musical Improv 401
(Diva Level!!!)

Musical Improv 401
Diva Level

Before we begin, I want to remind you that the skills we'll be working on in this section are quite advanced, and important if you desire to create the best songs possible (whether written or improvised.)

However.

If you are an improviser, please practice these skills and get comfortable with them before trying to perform them. Just as athletes practice certain skills over and over until muscle memory takes over, so they aren't consciously thinking about the mechanics of swinging a bat or throwing/catching a ball during a game, you should also practice and practice, so these musical skills can flow naturally on stage, rather than getting you more stuck in your head than before.

If you are a songwriter, my husband Marshall Stern's advice is simple: great lyrics are conversational, meaning that you would actually SAY them. If you aren't comfortable with these melodic and lyrical devices, they'll come across as you TRYING to be clever, which will come across as unnatural and stilted. Practice until they get a natural feel.

Remember Wu Wei, Baby! Effortless Effort!

~~~~

Chapter 11
Stephen Sondheim

I lead off the Diva section of this book with Sondheim, because he is widely acknowledged as a Master Songwriter, and if you can understand and use his techniques and style, you will truly be a musical improv Diva! Sondheim's music and lyrics are Art with a capital "A," which is hopefully what you want to achieve!

I used to teach "Sondheim" as a separate but equal song format to my performers in *MUSICAL! the musical*. I'd teach them Tagline, Verse-Chorus, and Sondheim. Format-wise, Sondheim uses verses and bridges and choruses, but they are more fluid than popular songs. If you are doing a more modern Broadway style for your show, I highly recommend getting accomplished in this style, since it really strikes a legitimate chord in the listeners!

That is not to say that these techniques are only for the musical theater style. Some of the most heralded popular songs use these melodic and lyrical tricks. You can do all the exercises in the next couple of chapters to the Sondheim-styled accompaniment tracks (which have a more musical theater and freeform feel), OR to the regular song format tracks which we have been using until this point.

Many books have been written on this master and his work, so forgive such a short chapter focusing on him. In reality, Chapters 12 and 13 are also included under the "Sondheim" umbrella. The verbal and melodic devices we learn in those chapters are excellent for standard songs formats as well as Sondheim-style songs. I'll keep this chapter to a brief Sondheim introduction so you can start improvising in his style, and you can continue to practice in the next chapters.

You really need to hear Stephen Sondheim's works to understand what I'm talking about and what you're trying to emulate. If you go to YouTube.com, simply search "Sondheim" and a TON of videos will come up. Best to watch professional productions, so you can get a good idea of how he's supposed to be performed!

Here are his shows (composer/lyricist except where noted):

* Saturday Night
* West Side Story (lyrics only)
* Gypsy (lyrics only)
* A Funny Thing Happened on the Way to the Forum
* Anyone Can Whistle
* Do I Hear a Waltz
* Company
* Follies
* A Little Night Music
* Pacific Overtures
* Sweeney Todd
* Merrily We Roll Along
* Sunday in the Park with George
* Into the Woods
* Assassins
* Passion
* The Frogs
* Road Show

Sondheim Lyrics, or the Wonderful World of Wordy Wordiness

Sondheim lyrics are often brilliant! If you study his lyrics, you may notice that he often uses:

* High emotion
* Internal rhymes
* Complex rhymes
* Alliteration, assonance and consonance
* Lists
* Many words (Listen to "Getting Married Today" from *Company*!)

High Emotion

Sondheim tends to be more emotionally charged than regular songs. On the emotional scale, Sondheim is the highest, as my high-tech bar graph demonstrates…

Song Emotionability

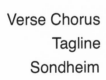

Of course, it's whatever you make it. I've heard some Verse Chorus songs that were very emotional, and some Sondheim-style songs that were emotionally neutral.

With Sondheim, it's as if his characters' subconscious emotions just rush out in song. When introduced to improvising Sondheim, I was told to use lots of staccato, bitter and biting lyrics. It works! But with more study, you learn that Sondheim is all about the incredible complexity of humanity, so the emotion in his songs has a vast range.

Emotional Sondheim Singing

Let's just jump in and start singing to Sondheim-style music. When you listen to it, you may hear a difference from the ordinary "song" accompaniment that we've been using so far. It sounds very modern musical theater. There's a lot going on, musically speaking.

Because Sondheim music tends to be complex and have a lot of notes, many singers get nervous and shy away from the style. In reality, it's a huge gift! WHATEVER you sing, it will probably fit with the complex chords, and even if it doesn't – great! It just makes it seem that much MORE complex!

This does not mean you can half hit notes and slide all around. Whatever you sing, do it with strong confidence. If you sorta hit a note and then slide to what the accompanist is playing, it will come across as a mistake. Whereas if you boldly hit a solid note, even if it's discordant with your accompanist, it will sound like it was written that way. (Especially if you hit that same note a few more times!)

As you sing, bring back words and phrases and motifs. Discover, explore, and heighten your lyrics and musical motifs!

Exercise 33 – Single Sondheim Emotion Verses

You'll use a Track from 41 to 44 , which are single verses in the Sondheim style. Just like the "Hearing the Emotion" Exercise 1 in Part 1, you're going to listen to the music and quickly discover the emotion and why your character is feeling that way (your situation). Then just start singing. It can be:

ᵡ Your internal thoughts

ᵡ What you're singing to someone in particular

ᵡ Telling a story that reflects or parallels what you're
experiencing right now

ᵡ Describing what your character is seeing/ hearing/ smelling/
feeling/ tasting/ smelling

Whatever. Just sing with all the emotion you can. If you're feeling
bitter, then make all your words bitter and biting. If you're feeling sad,
sing as morosely as possible, whatever that means to you! There's not
just one way to play "sad" or "angry," but if I could actually hear you, I
definitely would want to hear your sung words dripping with whatever
emotion you're singing in. It really helps to feel the emotion physically,
throughout your entire body. You'll find that you're less in your head
coming up with lyrics, and more feeling free and discovering the lyrics.

Play TRACKS 40-44 and do Exercise 33 now.

Exercise 34 - Wordiness Warm-up

I want you to time yourself for this. For one minute, talk as fast as
possible on any subject. (i.e. a childhood pet, a boyfriend/girlfriend,
an ex-boyfriend/girlfriend, a parent) Perhaps an angry, frightening,
or jealous memory. Some emotion that would have you speaking
quickly. Don't stop. If you don't know what to say, keep repeating
your last word or phrase until something else comes to mind. When
the first minute is up, now talk slowly (perhaps recalling a sad or
sweet memory of that pet, partner or parent) for the next minute.
Then switch back and forth between the fast talking and slow talking,
whenever you feel like it.

Do Exercise 34 now.

Exercise 35 – Double Sondheim Emotional Verses

As I said earlier, Sondheim is all about complexity. He understands that often a person feels really strongly about something, but then can turn on a dime and feel differently about it, too!

Play a Track from 45 to 46. Just as in the last exercise, listen to the music to discover your emotion, character and situation. Start singing in that emotion, justifying why you feel that way. After a verse, the music will change to a contrasting emotion. Immediately go with the music and sing about why you feel this new way about whatever your topic.

For example, if the music seems sweet and lovely to you, you may discover that your character is about to be married and is full of love and hope for the future. Perhaps you sing about the love of your life and how s/he sits and talks and behaves. Then the music switches to a very anxious, tense. You would immediately switch and sing about your love's behaviors that really tick you off. Or maybe how afraid you are of being shackled to someone. Whatever is in that new emotion about the same situation.

The music will return to the original emotion, and you'll switch back and explore more deeply why you feel that emotion (in our example, why you love this person, or why you are so hopeful.) Then it will switch to emotion number two. Go with it!

Don't just repeat what you said before, really discover new shades of your feelings and explore them.Use the last exercise as well – for one of the emotions, try singing as fast and as many words as possible, if it fits with the music and your emotion.

Play TRACKS 45-46 and do Exercise 35 now.

Nice! There's one other lyrical device that I want to cover before we move on.

Lists

Sondheim uses lists very often in his songs. It's a very natural way for people to think, which makes it easy and natural to use in improv songs. In his song "Agony" from *Into the Woods*, the singing Prince lists his wonderful attributes. In "Comedy Tonight" from *A Funny Thing Happened on the Way to the Forum*, the narrator lists what you'll see in the show. In "Another Hundred People" from *Company*, the singer lists off how people get to the city, where they meet and what they do there.

I think Sondheim was influenced by the earlier masters, Gilbert and Sullivan:

> His nose should pant
> and his lip should curl,
> His cheeks should flame
> and his brow should furl,
> His bosom should heave
> and his heart should glow,
> And his fist be ever ready
> for a knock-down blow.
>
> - Gilbert and Sullivan, "A British Tar," from *H.M.S. Pinafore,* 1878

And when talking about lists in songs, you can't forget what is known as "The List Song."

> There's the banjo serenader, and the others of his race,
> And the piano-organist — I've got him on the list!
> And the people who eat peppermint and puff it in your face,
> They never would be missed — they never would be missed!
> Then the idiot who praises, with enthusiastic tone,
> All centuries but this, and every country but his own;
> And the lady from the provinces, who dresses like a guy,
> And who "doesn't think she dances, but would rather like to try";
> And that singular anomaly, the lady novelist —
> I don't think she'd be missed — I'm sure she'd not he missed!
>
> - Gilbert and Sullivan, "As Someday it May Happen," from *The Mikado,* 1885

The first song lists the proper way for a British tar (sailor) to act, and the second is about an actual list the High Lord Executioner has of those whom he could execute if he ever needs a victim, since they'd never be missed.

Exercise 36 – Singing Lists

Let's sing some more in the Sondheim style, this time concentrating on lists. As always, play the music, listening to discover and feel the emotion. Discover the situation in context of a relationship. It may be with a parent, a child, a sibling, a teacher, a coworker, a lover or with yourself. Whatever the relationship, you feel a certain way towards this person as dictated by the emotion of the music. Start singing about this person, listing what s/he does to make you feel that way. Feel free to let the song evolve and throw in lists to whatever you're singing about!

Play TRACKS 40-46 and do Exercise 36 now.

This is merely a quick introduction to Sondheim style. I want you to be a bit familiar with it, as we move on to advanced melody and lyric work. Tracks 47-49 are full songs in the Sondheim style (Track 47 is a straight Tagline format), so you can include them when singing with subsequent exercises.

Chapter 12
Melody Rhythm and
Cadence 401

Advanced Melody: Working with Motifs

A motif is a short musical idea which is the building block of a musical work and therefore gives unity to a song or piece. In improv songs, I recommend that a motif should be between two and seven notes.

These small pieces of melody and rhythm appear repeatedly in a piece of music, sometimes exactly the same and sometimes changed. When a motif returns, it can be lower or higher in pitch, slower or faster, or in a different key. It may return "upside down" (with the notes going up instead of down, for example), or "mirrored," or altered in some other way.

One of the most famous motif is from the first movement of Beethoven's Symphony No. 5.

The rhythm is short short short loooong. The melody is three of the same notes, and then a drop down. (It drops down a third at first, but it changes, in some of the fun alterations that you do with motifs!)

You hear the motif (1 – the original motif) and then it is repeated a little lower (2):

Then Beethoven plays and has fun staggering the motif!

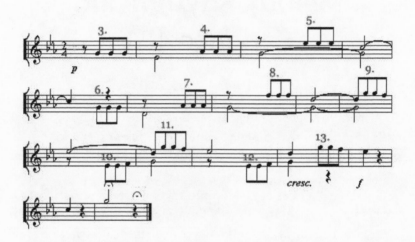

Play TRACK 50 now to hear a section of Beethoven's Fifth.

You can see and hear that he's repeating the motif, but making it more interesting by raising or lowering it, and making that drop down different - sometimes a third, sometimes only a half-step in motifs 3-8. Then, instead of having the first three notes exactly the same, he goes down on the third note in motif 9 (the notes start high and go down.). THEN he turns THAT upside-down by starting low and going up in motif 10! Wheee!

There's a fabulous video on YouTube that shows this score with a scrolling bar graph so you can SEE the motifs. It's titled "Beethoven, 5th Symphony" uploaded by Smalin.

So to recap, you have a 2-7 note motif. Remember it, because it's the building block, and you should return it occasionally during the song in its original form. But have fun and PLAY with the motif…

Raise or Lower It

Flip It UpsideDown

Flip It Backwards

Play with the Notes/Rhythm

Did you know: A motif thematically associated with a person, place or idea is called a leitmotif?

Q: Where do you find motifs?
A: Any number of places.

Sometimes the accompanist will play a little motif in his/her intro. (Some musicians do, and some don't, depending on how they learned and prefer to improvise.) Many people pick up on the motif when the musician plays one, but many people either don't hear it or prefer to use their own motif! Personally, I think it is a gift, like any offer in a scene, when the motif is supplied. Listen to it, then explore and heighten, as you would with any improv offer on stage.

If you have to come up with one on your own, you can use the natural melody of words and take it off the title, main theme or first words of the song. Remember Exercise 4, when you put those random words or phrases to music? Those can be motifs! So say they want you to sing a song about "belly button lint." You can take those five syllables and have an interesting 5-note motif. If you forget the motif, you can just sing those words out loud or in your mind and get it back. You can also use visual cues. Any shape around you can suggest notes on a scale.

For example, I have a deck player right at eye level if I look in front of me (the monitor's off to the side). There's a little logo that looks like this:

To me, this would be a three-note motif, short short long, all the same note. Now I told you to stay away from one-note melodies, and that's still true. But if I'm playing with my motif like I should be, I certainly won't stay on that note. I would raise it and lower it, and play around with it.

Here's another example. There are sunglasses on my desk. They look like this:

If I look along the top of the sunglasses, these points stand out for me

So I would sing a motif that follows those points –

If I were singing a song right here and forgot my motif, I could easily just glance at the sunglasses and remember it!

Of course, you might look at those sunglasses and see a totally different line, which would make a totally different motif. Both are right! How fabulous is that?!

Exercise 37A – Simple Two Note Motif Exercise

Let's start simply. Think of a two note motif. Remember, a motif has rhythm and melody. Perhaps your two note motif is *short* *long*, and it goes up a small step (not a big jump.) Sing it to Track 8 and experiment with it, singing it higher and lower, flipping it, and playing with rhythms and adding or subtracting notes.

Sing on "la la."

Since the music is the same over and over, you'll get some good practice in playing around with the motif. Return to the original motif now and again. **If you can't remember it, you strayed away from it too long.**

A live class is great for interaction. But this beats a class in that you can practice these exercises over and over until you not only are comfortable, but great at it!

Play TRACK 8 now and do Exercise 37A now.

Exercise 37B – Three and More Note Motifs

Do this exercise again with different three note motifs. Then a four note motif. Wow! You're going to be good at this! Remember, it's still on "la la."

Play TRACK 8 and do Exercise 37B

Exercise 38 – Musical Motifs to a Full Verse

Now let's sing motifs in a slightly more realistic way. Play Tracks 11-15 or Sondheim music Tracks 41-44 and do exercise 37A and 37B again. This time, the music plays full verses, giving typical chord progressions. This actually makes it easier for you to play with your motif, because if the music goes to a different place, all you have to do is follow it, and your motif will go to a different place, too.

At first, just try singing your motif higher and lower to the music. You'll probably have to add or subtract notes at the end of the fourth line, so it sounds like your melody is ending with the music.

When you're comfortable with that, try changing your motif around in more fun ways (flipping it, singing it backwards, whatever...) fitting it in with the music.

You can sing to these tracks over and over and over, since your motif will be different each time.

You're still singing on "la la," and not words yet.

You know that example I did on Track 10? It sounded like a real song because I used a motif. Go back and listen to it again. Do you hear the motif? Do you hear how I changed it? Do you hear that I used it and still ended the verse so it sounded like it was ending?

Play TRACK 10 for an example.

Play TRACKS 11-15, 41-44 and do Exercise 38 now.

Rhythm and Cadence – Where Music Meet Lyrics

The combination of the melody, rhythm, and lyrics is the cadence, or phrasing. When the phrasing of the lyrics - the natural melody and rhythm of the words - fits with the melody and rhythm of the music, we got some good stuff going!

You've got musical motifs down. Now to start putting words to them.

Two Note Motifs

Let's take a two-note motif. Best to look at it as syllables. Two syllables are usually

Iambic

˘ / (You can also think of this as "da DUM" or "short long" or "unstressed stressed" or "not accented, accented." Also known as an iambic foot.)

Or

Trochaic

/ ˘ ("DUM da", "long short" or "stressed unstressed" or accented, not accented)

(It could be two stressed or two unstressed in a row, but that's hard to maintain for any length of time!)

Now, once you get started, Iambic and Trochaic are fairly similar. They both alternate between accented and not accented syllables. Once you get good at one, you'll get good at the other, too! We'll get to the difference later on.

Shakespeare used iambic pentameter. (Five feet of unstressed stressed - you know, "pent" means five as in "pentagon.")

˘ / ˘ / ˘ / ˘ / ˘ /

Da DUM - da DUM - da DUM - da DUM - da DUM

When I - do count - the clock - that tells - the time (Shakespeare's 12th Sonnet)

Exercise 39 – Iambic Speaking

Get the "da DUM, da DUM, da DUM" rhythm in your head and start speaking, trying to fit what you say into that rhythm. For example,

I'm SIT-ting ON the COUCH and TYP-ing FAS-cin-NAT-ing STUFF.

Keep it up for as long as you can, and notice when it starts getting easier and more natural to do.

Switch to "DUM da, DUM da" rhythm and see if there's any difference.

Do Exercise 39 now.

> ∿∽∿∽∿∽
>
> Being able to improvise in certain rhythms is a great skill! Not only is it wonderful for your songs, but certain styles have certain rhythms. As already noted, Shakespeare used iambs. So if you can speak with a "da DUM da DUM" rhythm, it really reads very Shakespearean. Especially because your words will be slightly awkward to fit the rhythm, so instead of speaking normally with a "thee" or "-est" thrown in as most improvisers do, you're closer to the true style and don't have to rely on tricks or gags. Instead of saying, "Stop bothering me!" you have the rhythm "da DUM" in your head and may say, "oh, such a bother! Stop, I say!" which is sooooo much better for the style!
>
> ∽∿∽∿∽∿

Exercise 40A – Iambic Speaking to Music

Excellent. Now I want you to play any of the tracks 11-15 (aren't you sick of these tracks by now?!) and speak in this same way to the music. It's as if you were singing, but you're just speaking. You can fill four beats and rest for four beats, or fill the entire line. You can speak slowly or quickly. But know when each line is starting, so you can start with it. Try not to just ramble on and on. Treat the words as the lyrics to this tune, with each line being a whole unit.

Singing quickly might be:

Please <u>PASS</u> me <u>ALL</u> the <u>RAI</u>-sin-<u>ETTES</u>, they <u>REAL</u>-ly <u>ARE</u> so <u>GOOD</u>

where the underlined syllables are on the beat.

Singing slower (with a beat between each phrase) could be:

Please <u>PASS</u> [<u>rest</u>] me <u>ALL</u> [<u>rest</u>] the <u>RAI</u> [<u>rest</u>] sin-<u>ETTES</u> [<u>rest</u>]

If you try going fast and just can't keep up, then slow down and go at the speed you're comfortable with. Eventually speed up, just to gain the skill. I think improvisers tend to go too quickly, and could really benefit from slowing down their lyrics. But to be ABLE to sing quickly when needed is a great skill. So work on both!

Play TRACKS 11-15 and do Exercise 40A now.

Exercise 40B - Forward Rhyming, Iambic Speaking to Music

When you get good at Exercise 40A, try rhyming. Do an **aabb** type of forward rhyme.

Play TRACKS 11-15 and do Exercise 40B now.

Exercise 40C – Setting Up Rhymes, Iambic Speaking to Music

When you get good at THAT (Exercise 40B), set up your rhyming couplets.

Play TRACKS 11-15 and do Exercise 40C now.

Fabulous. You know what to do next. You got it – SING it!

Singing Rhythmic Words to Make Motifs

A stressed or accented syllable is higher in pitch than an un-stressed or unaccented one. Say your name out loud. If it has more than one syllable, then you'll hear it. NAN-cy. The "nan" is higher than the "cy." If your name is Pierre, then you probably say it pee-AIR, which is lower and then higher in pitch. (Tee hee! I said "Pee!")

Remember, a motif has:

* **The Shape**. In a two-note motif, that means does it go up or down? (I'm trying to keep you away from one-note melodies.) In higher number note motifs, you can see the shape of the motif by the actual notes on the sheet music. Remember when I had you moving your finger up and down to your melody in Part 1? That was good practice to recognize the shape of what you sing! If you're trying to follow the melody of the words you're using, you don't have much choice on whether the pitches go up or down. The pitches are already in the words. You DO have a choice on...

* **The Intervals**. In a two-note motif, there's just one interval between the notes, since there are only two notes. The interval is how much the notes jump up or down. This is totally up to you. If I were to sing my name as a motif, I know that wherever I start, my second note is going to be lower (remember, accented syllable are higher, or it just doesn't scan right.) My second note might drop just a little, perhaps a half note, or it could drop hugely, like an entire octave.

⨯ The Rhythm. Notes can be long and held out or short and stac-cato. A song can sound completely different if you change the rhythm. Remember in Beethoven's Fifth, the motif rhythm was short-short-short-loooooong. Think of those same notes, but done loooong-short-loooong-short. That's a totally different motif!

Exercise 41 – Singing Two-Note Motifs

You've already practiced singing motifs on "la la." Now you're going to put words to it. Easy Peasy, since we practiced speaking in two-note cadence motifs as well. For this exercise, choose a motif to start with. Since we're starting with two-note motifs, decide if your motif is going up or down, and how big an interval between the two notes. Play a track from 11-15 or 40-42. If your motif is going up, then you're doing a da-DUM type of accent/stress, since stressed syllables are higher in pitch. If going down, you're doing a DUM-da type.

Sing words that fit the accented syllable naturally, and fit in with the music. If you have decided to do a motif that goes up just one step between notes, for example, that doesn't mean every time you sing exactly the same notes. You get to play with the motif group. You can move the group of notes (in this case just two notes) up, or down. Feel free to end each line - and especially the verse - naturally, which may mean you take out or add a syllable or two. (If you listen to my motif example on Track 8 singing on "la la," you'll notice that the motif does change, especially at the end of lines.)

To begin, it may be easier to start by just speaking a couple of lines that fit your motif rhythm, like in the last exercise, to get the rhythm into your head. Then start singing. (If you're having trouble, simply repeat the lines you just spoke and then continue singing new lyrics.) You may want to practice singing words to motifs without worrying about rhyming at first. When you get comfortable doing that, try forward rhyming. When you get comfortable with that, try setting up your rhymes.

Note: Since it is a two-note group, it should feel like there is a comma (or even a period) between groups. It's not just a run-on sentence of da-DUM-da-DUM-da-DUM-da-DUM. It's da DUM, da-DUM, da-DUM, da-DUM.

You'll notice that the motif groups have to make sense unto themselves. If you are thinking of a two-note motif that goes down (DUM-da), and thinking of it as a run-on sentence, you may be tempted to sing something like:

(To) BE or NOT to BE that IS the QUES-tion.

That makes no sense if it's a "DUM-da" two-note motif. It would come out like:

(to) BE or, NOT to, BE that, IS the, QUES-tion.

If you're doing a two-note motif, it makes WAY more sense to have a da-DUM of:

To BE, or NOT, to BE, that IS, the QUEST(tion.)

Play TRACKS 11-15, and/or 41-44 and do Exercise 41 now.

Higher Note Motifs

Now say we had a four-note motif that sounded like da-DUM-da DUM. (The second and fourth notes are higher than the first and third.) You can do really fun things with rhythm, once you get more notes going. The rhythm is totally up to you. I just bring this up to show the difference between this and a two-note da-DUM motif. A two-note motif words might be:

You SIT. You WATCH. You SEE, the WORLD.

In a four-note motif, the phrasing would be different:

You SIT and WATCH. You SEE the WORLD.

So think of the words in groups or phrases that match your cadence motif and melody/pitch.

Exercise 42 – Speaking More Complicated Cadence Motifs

If you can do this exercise, then singing the words will come very easily. We've already practiced speaking two-note motifs. Now you're going to practice putting words to the syllables. Remember, these are phrases, so if you are doing the first DUM-da-da cadence motif, each phrase will be three syllables long, fitting the DUM-da-da, DUM-da-da, DUM-da-da, DUM-da-da cadence motif.

Practice speaking in these cadence motifs:

-DUM-da-da
(i.e. "WHY are you, SUCH a good, FRIEND of mine?")

-da-DUM-da
(i.e. "i ASK you, to GIVE me, a SAND-wich, of PORK rinds."

-da-da-DUM
(i.e. "cab-a-RET, is the BEST, form of FUN, that there IS!"

-da-DUM-da-da-DUM
(i.e. "i LOVE that you THINK, i'm NOTH-ing but SMART")

-da-DUM-da-DUM
(i.e. "i REAL-ly HATE, your FREAK-in' GUTS, i WANT to STAB, you IN the NUTS!")

-da-da-da-DUM
(i.e. "i really HATE, your freakin' GUTS, i want to STAB, you in the NUTS!")

Did you notice those last two are the same exact words? They fit for both! It's not magic - it just depends on how you sing them! That's not to say you can sing anything and force it to fit. You will hear if your lyrics sound natural or not. Make them natural. It's as simple as that!

Make up your own cadence motifs! (Exercise 22, where we made up Limericks, had us putting words in a "da-DUM-da-da-DUM-da-da-DUM-(da)" type cadence.)

Pick a cadence motif, and speak words to it for as long as you can. Get comfortable and confident, knowing that this isn't so hard. Once you get good, speak in lines that rhyme.

Do Exercise 42 now.

> Please note: I'm using the term "cadence motif" to describe motifs that have a certain accented/unaccented order. I'll stick to that for simplicity's sake, since it leaves the specific rhythm open to your own choice. If you prefer to assign yourself more rhythmic motifs that make sense to you (i.e. "dah deedle dum"), have at it!

Exercise 43 - Putting it All Together – Singing Motifs

Pick a topic or title from the appendix. Pick a cadence motif to begin. The first time that you do this, speak the first two lines to the music and then start singing on the third line. Once you know that you CAN do it, just start singing from the get go! Again, if rhyming is troubling you, start with NO rhymes until you're comfortable, then forward rhyme, then set up your rhymes.

Play TRACKS 11-15 and 41-44 (Sondheim) for one verse of practice, 18-22 and 45-46 (Sondheim) for two or more verses, and then 25-29 for Tagline full songs, 35-39 for Verse Chorus full songs, 47-49 for full Sondheim style songs, and do Exercise 43 now.

♪ ♪ ♪

Chapter 13
Pleasing Sound Lyrics 401

For most improvisers, words are just a way to get a laugh. Words are what need to be spoken or sung to fill the space and the silence. But for you who are reading Part 4 (Congratulations on making it this far!), you obviously want to be great at musical improv or songwriting, and can see beyond the Craft into the potential of ART! For this, you must understand the following:

Words are also SOUNDS.

Simple, eh? But as I said, they are not treated as such by the vast majority of improvisers and songwriters out there. Words have sound and shape and innate emotions behind them.

My husband, a very talented songwriter, says that when words come before emotion, the lyrics are dead. So true! When emotion comes first, and you discover the words from that, the lyrics are living! If your character is sad, and you're feeling that emotion, then the sounds/words you discover will sound sad. The images you discover will convey sadness. Your listener will share sadness with you. If you're in your head, not feeling sad, but trying to come up with sad or funnily sad lyrics, the words might technically mean something sad, but they won't be alive and they won't give listeners the experience of connecting with your sadness.

Discover the Words

Improv is best when you take your brain out of it (a.k.a. "getting out of your head") and discover what is happening organically. This is how the brilliant stuff happens. The Art. The same can be said of lyrics – you can get stuck up in your head, trying to figure out the most clever word/phrase/rhyme, or you can relax and just discover what's there. Of course, to do this, you must be emotionally invested in whatever is happening, so that there IS something to discover.

If you are singing the blues and you need to sing a verse about spiders, for example, you need to go into whatever emotion you're feeling. If it's fear, go into it and FEEL it, because if you do, you'll discover that images and/or sounds are right there! (As opposed to going into your head and not being connected, so you have to THINK about being scared of spiders.) Thinking about spiders is once removed from feeling about spiders. The closer you are emotionally to your topic, the more you can simply discover the lyrics.

Exercise 44 – Discovering Words Through Emotion

This exercise is a near repeat of Exercise 1 from Part 1, but focused on discovering through the emotion. Here are the steps:

* Play a Track 2-6, or 41-44.

* FEEL the emotion evoked by the music, mentally and physically.

* Discover why your character feels this way.

* Sing about what your character is experiencing right now with his/her senses that reinforce that emotion. For example, if your character is angry at their spouse for being uncaring, you might discover that you're in the kitchen and sing about the dishes piled in the sink that he said he'd wash, and the ticket to Vegas on the counter so he can have a fun weekend with the boys while you stay with the kids. Discover everything that you

see that makes you feel your emotion. The emotion should cause you to discover what you see, but each discovery should reinforce and increase the emotion, which causes you to discover more things. You don't have to stay on sight. Discover sounds and smells that echo what you feel.

If you find yourself in your head trying to think of what you are seeing/hearing/smelling/etc., you're working too hard! Go into the emotion and really feel it. Discovery is way easier (and inspired) than consciously coming up with ideas.

Play TRACK 2-6, or 41-44 and do Exercise 44 now.

Emotional Sounds

I'm not just talking about onomatopoeia here (words that imitate actual sounds - like "kersplatt" or "meow.") I'm talking about words (which are symbols for actual things/events/states/etc.) that are based on emotional sound. For example, asked to list as many words as possible that "sound happy" to me, I may say, "happy, glee, joy, wheee!, celebration," etc. Notice the preponderance of the "ee" sound in there. I remember hearing that REM wrote the song "Shiny Happy People" with so many "ee" sounds so people would have to smile when singing it.

As we've just seen in the last exercise, it's fairly easy for people to get words from images – an emotion is felt, and certain images come to mind, which means we can verbalize and sing about them. Sweet! It's almost automatic!

In this exercise, however, we're practicing getting in touch with the emotion of the sound. This is tough for many people. Don't worry if it's hard for you – just getting this concept in your head so it percolates will make you a better wordsmith.

Oh. And you may not want to do this exercise when others are within hearing range…

Exercise 45 – Sound Symbols

I'll give you some emotional or states-of-being words. At first, I want you just to make sounds that match up emotionally to the word you're doing. Try a lot of sounds and see what are best. You can go through the alphabet if you want to, just testing all the sounds out. Don't forget blending sounds together like "bl" "cr" and "sh." Then come up with words with those sounds and list them off.

For example, if the word is "contented," I would first try to emotionally feel contented, then (out loud) try sounds and see which ones match my emotion and make me feel even more contented. In other words, what are "contented" sounds? Start with vowel sounds, and then do consonants. For me, my top ones would be "ahhh" "oooh" "mmmmm," but "ffff" "hhhh" "jjjj" "lllll" "sssss" "vvvv" and "zzzzz" also echo my contented feeling. I bet some of these sounds would be the same for you, and that you would also have different ones. Fine! We are going for sounds that resonate with you RIGHT NOW. Be present with your emotion and your sounds, and your words will be alive!

Now use these sounds to discover words. Just start making the sounds and see what word starts forming or comes out... mmmmmmaaaaahhmmmmmmm... oh! Mama! Look at that! That IS a very contented word! Aaaahhhhhhhmmmmmmmmm......amish! Hmmm...I suppose "Amish" can be contented. Here's a short list of mine when I do this exercise to "contented."

Mama

Amish

Oz

Safe

Fool

Jell-O

Mahmoud Ahmadinejad

Okay. Well, I wouldn't say "fool" or "Ahmadinejad" is the first thing I THINK of when you say "contented," but they have many of my contented sounds in them! I can imagine a contented song that has those words.

Point is, don't judge your words, just make as many as you can with the sounds you feel that particular emotional connection with. Those unusual words can be BRILLIANT in a song, since they are not the same old tired thing that everyone else thinks of!

Here are some emotional words you can practice with:

Lazy

Joyous

Bright

Dull

Sharp

Caress

Death

Dance

Do Exercise 45 now.

Exercise 46 – Singing Sound Symbols

Play Track 2-6 or Tracks 41-44 again. Listen to the music and feel the emotion of it. Now just sing random words that really show the emotion. It's what we just did in Exercise 45, but instead of the impetus coming from a word I gave, you have the music, and instead of just listing the words, you're singing them.

Play TRACKS 2-6, 41-44 and do Exercise 46 now.

Pleasing Sounds, Lyrically Speaking

Good lyrics have a pleasing sensation of sound. This includes:

* **Rhyming** (similar sound at the end of the words – accented syllable on)

* **Alliteration** (similar sound at the start of the words) "What a Wonderful World"

* **Consonance** (similar consonant sounds internally in the words) "some mammals are clammy"

* **Assonance** (similar vowel sounds), as in "few consumers want to neuter the future of Winnie the Pooh - do you?"

Say those phrases out loud. They ARE pleasing!

Internal Rhyming

Rhyming is the master of pleasing sounding lyrics. We've been all over this one, and you've been doing it for most of the book. But let's step it up a notch and practice *internal* rhyming.

You know how to do this – rhymes inside the line, rather than just at the end of the line. Sondheim uses it a lot. In fact, I just wrote a couplet with internal rhymes on FaceBook:

> If you're **blessed** with all your money, but **obsessed** with what is owed
> Don't be **hateful** of the pothole, be **grateful** for the road!
> - Nancy Howland Walker, FaceBook Status Update , 2012

And don't forget the classic:

> Strolling with my **girlie** where the dew is **pearly early** in the morning,
> Butterflies all **flutter up** and kiss each little **buttercup** at dawning
> - "G. Kahn and W. Donaldson, "Carolina in the Morning," 1922

Exercise 47 - Internal Rhyme Story

Tell a story, rhyming as often in a row as you can. When you say a major word that doesn't rhyme, switch to rhyming THAT word. For example…

> A fat cat sat on a heater. Couldn't be sweeter, but I forgot to feed her. So she died, on her wide side. I lied to my mother who loved no other than the cat and my brother. So she smothered me. Do you see? Wheee!

Do Exercise 47 now.

Exercise 48 - Internal Rhyme Story in Rhythm

Now do that same story (or a new one) to any rhythm you choose. For example to (da) DUM da da DUM…

> A CAT that was FAT, once she SAT on a HEATer. Nothing SWEETer, didn't FEED her, so she DIED on her SIDE that was WIDE. So I LIED to my MOTHer, not aNOTHer or my BROTHer. I was SMOTHered. Do you SEE? That was ME. I say WHEEE!

Stay as close to your rhythm as you can while having the words flow. (In other words, don't torture yourself with strict adherence to the rhythm to where it's making you feel bad if you stray a little bit. Challenge yourself. Stretch yourself. But don't defeat yourself!)

Do Exercise 48 now.

Exercise 49 – Internal Rhyme Story in Verse Form

Now practice doing that same story (or a new one) in a verse form, with four or eight beats per line

A CAT that was FAT, once she SAT on a HEATer
She DIED on her SIDE that was WIDE – didn't FEED her.

Do Exercise 49 now.

Exercise 50 - Complex Internal Rhymes

Tell a new story, but this time use more complex rhymes. As we saw in Part 1, an easy way to do this is to rhyme the adjective before the noun. So rather than just rhyming "cat" with "bat" and "hat," we might have a "DOMESTIC cat" rhyming with a "MAJESTIC cat." Tell a story, using as many complex rhymes as possible.

Do Exercise 50 now.

Exercise 51 – Lots of Rhymes to Music

Let's practice singing Sondheim with tons of rhymes. Pick a subject from the following list of typical Sondheim themes:

Love/Hate
Marriage
Death
Conflict
Aging
Disillusionment (with the Arts, with parents, with politicians – whatever!)

Play a Sondheim style musical track, making sure to get into the emotion, and start singing, rhyming as much as you can. Just like we've been doing in the last few exercises.

Play TRACKS 41-49 and do Exercise 51 now.

Alliteration

This is one of the most obvious of pleasing sounds. That's why it's everywhere, from stores (Circuit City, Best Buy), cartoon characters and superheroes (Mickey Mouse, Donald Duck, Peter Parker, Lois Lane, Clark Kent), News headlines ("Credit Crunch Crime Wave" "Saucy Sarah's Sex Secrets with Secretary of State"), and expressions ("good as gold," "dead as a doornail")

> To sit in solemn silence in a dull, dark dock,
> In a pestilential prison, with a life-long lock,
> Awaiting the sensation of a short, sharp shock,
> From a cheap and chippy chopper on a big black block!
> - Gilbert and Sullivan, "I am so Proud," *The Mikado*, 1885

Alliteration is pretty powerful because it pounds into our brainpan. It's a tiptop and tantalizing and trustworthy tool. A distinguished, desirable and dependable device! A fine phenomenon that...oh, you get it!

In case you come across the word "Sibilance," it is just referring to a specific kind of alliteration using the softer consonants that have a hissing (or sibilant) sound. These include the sounds: s, sh, th, ch, z, f, and x.

Exercise 52 – Speaking Alliteration

Let's get great at discovering alliterations...

Exercise 52A – Speaking Short Alliterative Phrases

Look around you, and notice any object. And just give it a descriptive word that starts with the same sound. For example, I see a "Terrible Television!" And a "Frustrating Phone," a "Crazy Cat," a "Lovely Lake," (it's right out my window), a "Rank Rug," and a "Pretty Picture."

They don't all have to be an alliterative description of the object name. It could be a phrase of what I'm experiencing. For example, a

"Terrible Time-Sucker" (the television) or an "Insolent Interruption" (the telephone.) Or take the alliteration sound off the description and re-name the object. My jeans look dirty, so instead of taking the "j" sound, I can take the "d" sound – "Dirty Dungarees."

Do Exercise 52A now.

Exercise 52B – Speaking Longer Alliterative Phrases

I'll give you an emotion/feeling and a sound. Try to make a sentence, or at least a phrase, with as many words as you can come up with that start with that sound. When you run out of words with that sound, continue the thought or sentence and change to another beginning sound.

For example: if excitement and the sound "wh" were given to me, I might say…

> When and why and where will we wander? Whisking off to (here I've run out of w sounds, so I switch) beaches. Bound in bikinis, bouncing breasts and bottoms, beach ball play and perilous pleasures…etc…

Keep going, switching your alliterative sound whenever you run out of the one you're doing. At first it will be awkward and slow, but try to get faster and have the sentences make sense.
Here are your suggestions:

Emotion –	Sound
Anger	p
Fear	k (remember, a hard "c" is a "k" sound)
Sadness	d
Love	f
Disgust	r
Surprise	w
Remorse	g
Optimistic	h

Remember, it's based on the sound, not the letter.

Do Exercise 52B now.

Exercise 53 – Speaking Alliteration in Rhythm

Go back to the above list of emotions and sounds. Do the same exercise, but this time speak out loud to specific cadence motif rhythms. It's fine if you remember and use some of the same words you already used. They'll change because now you're fitting them into a rhythm. Fine if you can't remember what you said and make up totally new words! You'll find that the accented syllables are usually the ones that naturally get the strong alliteration sounds.

For example, if I were to do my example from the previous exercise (excitement to the "w" sound - which I only remember because it's written there) to the cadence motif rhythm of "da DUM da da" it might turn out to be, " oh WHEN will we, and WHY will we, and WHERE will we, go WANDer now? Soon WHISKing off, to BEACHes hot, and BOUNDing in, biKINis – not! The BOUNcing breasts, and BOTtoms hard, play BEACHball with, their BODy guard."

Feel free to change what you did before – and feel free to rhyme, if it's right there. Don't go out of your way to rhyme for right now – do it once you're comfortable with just speaking alliterations in rhythm.

Try using Exercise 52 alliterations to the following cadence motifs:

DUM da da

da da DUM

da DUM da

DUM da DUM da

da DUM da da DUM

Do Exercise 53 now.

Exercise 54– Singing Alliteration

Very good. Now play any of the music tracks and sing your sentences or phrases from Exercise 53. It doesn't matter if you remember what exactly you said before. Of course, you can do brand new lyrics if you want. I just want you to sing alliterations (hopefully from emotion) to a specific rhythm, which will suggest a motif, which becomes an awesome melody!

Play TRACKS 11-15, 18-22, 41-49 and do Exercise 54 now.

Consonance

Consonance is very much like alliteration, because it's based on the repetition of consonant sounds. (In fact, just like squares and rectangles, all alliteration is consonance, but not all consonance is alliteration!) When I talk about consonance, I mean repetition of consonant sounds throughout the words – at the beginning, middle, and/or end. Whereas alliteration is repetition of consonant sounds only at the beginning of words.

> **Du**m**b Ji**mm**y ca**m**e ho**m**e, **m**u**m**bling about **m**ore ha**m**burger **m**eat.

Yay! That's a lot of mmmm sound! Alliteration is definitely more obvious to the ear, but consonance is satisfying, too.

Exercise 55 – Consonance Practice

Pick a consonant sound. You can go through the alphabet and choose. (For those a little behind in grammar terms, there are 5 vowels – a,e,i,o,u [and sometimes "y"!] – the rest of the letters in the alphabet are consonants!) Don't forget blends of consonants, like bl, cr, sc, etc. Make a sentence with words that have lots of that sound, just like I did with the "mm" sound above. Do this with different consonant sounds until you get comfortable and fairly fast at doing it.

Do Exercise 55 now.

Exercise 56 – Singing Consonance

Pick a topic from Appendix D. Sing a verse about that topic in an **aabb** rhyme scheme. Before you start singing, decide on your two landing words, as well as the two rhyming words you'll use to set up those landing words. Use the beginning letters or the letters of the stressed syllables in your chosen words as your consonance sound in that line.

For example, if I picked the topic "night," the two associated landing words that immediately pop into my head are "tired" and "nocturnal." Picking rhymes to set up those words, I choose "wired" and "infernal."

So I'll use as many "w" sounds as possible in the first line, since it will end on "wired." I'll use lots of "t" sounds in the second line, since it will end on "tired." The third line will end on "infernal," so I can either have as many "in" sounds or "f" sounds, since those are the starting sound and the stressed syllable sound. I choose "f." Then "n" for nocturnal. I could chose "t" since the stressed syllable starts with that, but I already have a "t" line. Remember, this is just for practice. For this exercise I'm forcing you to set up your rhymes and do a full line of consonance. In a real song, consonance can be used in just a phrase, or the sound can change a couple of times during a line if you're using this tool.

_____(many "w" sounds)_____	wired
_____(many "t" sounds)_____	tired
_____(many "f" sounds)_____	infernal
_____(many "n" sounds_____	nocturnal

Singing my verse might sound something like:

> When power women slave away, we are so awfully wired
> Titanic restorative stimulants keep from being tired
> The buffet of quick fix Redbull and flowing drugs infernal
> Have turned me nightly thin skinned and now I am nocturnal.

Phew! That's hard for me to not JUST do alliterations! This is difficult for most people, so don't give up – start with just a couple of the sounds per line, and then sprinkle more in as you practice.

Play TRACKS 11-15, 18-22, 41-49 and do Exercise 56 now.

Assonance

I've heard this called "vowel rhyme," since the stressed vowel sounds (and sometimes the following unstressed vowel sounds) are the same. If the consonants are close, it can be considered a "near" or "Nashville" rhyme. But the consonants don't have to be the same or close – just the vowel sounds. For example:

> **Sw**ee**t** dr**ea**ms
> H**i**t or m**i**ss

Exercise 57 – Simple Assonance

I'm calling just one vowel sound being repeated "simple" assonance. I'll give you a vowel sound, and you come up with a sentence that has as many of the stressed (and unstressed, if you can!) vowels as possible in that sound.

As always, it's not based on spelling, but on sound. Since you're reading this, you may get the spelling in your head and think of only words with those letters. Really try to go just on sound. For example, if I give you the sound "er," you may think "fern" and "herb." If I give the sound "ur," you may think "burn" or "burp." If I write "ir," you may come up with "skirt" or "firm." All great words, but all the SAME assonance! So as you're practicing, notice if you're stuck on a particular spelling in your head, or rhyming rather than doing assonance. (If you just come up with "burn, spurn, learn" those are rhymes – change the final sound from an "n" to something else.)

If I give the "er" sound, a sentence could be

"Your firm burp spurred me to burn your fertile germs.

One – I could say "your" like "yer" and have even MORE assonance, and two – okay, it doesn't make a ton of sense, but that's fine!

This exercise will probably be slow going at first, but as with everything, the more you practice, the better, faster and more natural it becomes.

Here are your sounds:

er (hey, it's in your brain right now!)

ih – as in "kiss"

eye – as in "island"

ar – as in "party"

oo – as in "fool"

uh – as in "bummer"

ay – as in "aids"

ow – as in "ow"

Keep going, picking and practicing your own vowel sounds.

I find that when I do this, I automatically put in rhyming and/or alliteration, since it's right there in my mind. Fabulous, if that happens, but don't TRY to force it. ("Picking an icky pickle is hit or miss in Piccadilly Circus," was my "ih" sound one.) These sentences are usually very funny - have fun!

Do Exercise 57 now.

Exercise 58 – Complex Assonance

Now that you have simple assonance in your ears and head, let's take it one step further. Let's do TWO vowel sounds! Wheee! It will be the accented vowel and the vowel after it. The consonants in between and after can be completely different. (If they're not, that's more of a rhyme.)

Assonance, especially complex assonance, is very important in hip-hop/rap. If you're going to try improvising in this style, getting good at this will make your rap soooooo much better!

For example, Public Enemy uses the line:

Their pens and pads I snatch 'cause I've had it.

and "assonance rhyme" it with the line:

I'm not an addict, fiending for static

in their song "Don't Believe the Hype." "Had it," "addict," and "static" are complex assonances, and in the next lines, Public Enemy also uses the assonance words "have it," "grab it," and "rabbit"

The complex assonance here is "a" (as in "badass") and then "ih" (as in "hymn"). The "a" is stressed and the "ih" is not. So if you get the "DUM-da" rhythm in your head, and replace it with "A- ih" and try to come up with words, you might get "manic" "bandit," "happen," etc.

List as many words (out loud) as you can come up with that fit these vowel sounds, making sure not to just rhyme, but to change the consonants up.

After you've said the list of words, go back and put them and any others that might come to you into a sentence. It should make grammatical sense, but don't worry if it doesn't make logical sense. (See examples below of actual songs!)

Here are your sounds:

A - ih (as in "attic")

EE - ih (as in "dreamin'")

EYE – er (as in "miser")

IH – er (as in "killer")

OR – ee (as in "morning")

After you do those, come up with your own, just starting a sentence out loud, and riffing on any word or words you say.

Do Exercise 58 now.

Exercise 59 – Even More Complex Assonance

In the song "Triumph," Inspectah Deck begins his section with lots of assonance:

I bomb atomically – Socrates' philosophies and hypotheses

and follows it with:

can't define how I be droppin' these mockeries.

That's a lot of complex assonance!

Then there's "Earl" by Earl Sweatshirt, that uses this kind of complex assonance, saying he's an:

astronaut crashing while jacking off to bufferings vids of...

and of course the vids have the same complex assonance:

Asher Roth eating apple sauce.

Wow. Mr. Deck is closer to near rhymes than Mr. Sweatshirt, but both are using assonance in a "DUM da da" or "DUM da DUM" rhythm (depending on how you say it!) The middle syllable changes, but the first and last are the same, assonance-wise.

The Inspectah has "Ah- __ -ee(z)" (S**ocrates**, droppin' th**ese**, m**ockeries**)

and the Earl has "A- __ -aw" (**A**stron**aut**, **A**sher Roth, **a**pple s**auce**)

Keep on going and add more lines to these songs with the assonances they started.

Then try ones that match these phrases:

ARM and hand

TURpentine

Internet

SENsible (the "ble" has an implied "**uh**" sound – like sensibull!)

Keep going, starting your own sentence and riffing off a word that comes up.

Do Exercise 59 now.

Fabulous! If you get really good at this, your rhyming will be phenomenal, because you'll be able to do near and unexpected rhymes fairly easily.

Easy Combos

Rhyming, Alliteration, Consonance, and Assonance are amazingly wonderful tools for the songwriter (instant or not). The great wordsmiths use them – poets and songwriters, speechwriters, rappers, and poetry slam artists. Much of the time, writers don't use just one of these tools, they use more. (As I said before, if you practice these, then it will come naturally, since your brain will just hear it.) Sometimes it's even easier to combine them.

Pararhymes (Alliteration and Consonance)

"**D**aw**n** goes **d**ow**n**" – Robert Frost, "Nothing Gold Can Stay," 1923

All you do for this combination is change the vowel sound. You can do that easily for most one-syllable words that start and end in a consonant. Let's try it - just looking around my room, I see a phone (My phone was fine – a fan in the fen found it.), a clock (The clock went click and clack, but didn't cluck.), and a door (The dear door was dire on a dare.) Yup, it works and is really easy. The sentences I made up don't make the most sense, but they'd be great in a song!

Exercise 60 – Pararhyme Practice

Look around your room and discover any one-syllable object that starts and ends with a consonant. Then just make up a sentence by keeping those consonants and changing the middle vowel sound.

Do Exercise 60 now.

Alliteration and Assonance

Also fairly easy, because you start the word and just discover what's right there. It comes across as a more intense alliteration, since the first couple of sounds (rather than only the first sound) are the same.

"**Su**nny **Su**mmer" – Robert Frost, "The Silken Tent," 1939

Again, looking around the room I see a "picture," so I start most of my words with a "pih" sound…

"**Pi**cking a **pi**cture of a **pi**ll will **pi**ss the **pi**g off!"

When I do this, I just start the word with the sound and discover the rest of the word. It's not a matter of thinking of the words ahead of time. Trust that the rest of the word will come. But you've got to start the word. Out loud. Try it.

Exercise 61 – Alliteration and Assonance Practice

Say these sounds out loud and make them into a word. No wrong answer as long as the word is real (for this exercise – feel free to make up your own words under emergency circumstances. I have been known to make up names in rhyme emergencies – "silver?" Meet "Professor Pilver!")

Turn these sounds into as many words as you can (spelling doesn't matter)...

> dee...
>
> quih...
>
> meye...

Now look around you and pick out an object that starts with a consonant. Say it out loud to hear the first consonant and vowel sound of the word. Then make up a sentence that has as many words that start with those sounds as possible.

Do Exercise 61 now.

Exercise 62 – Combo Practice to Rhythms

Pick a cadence motif rhythm and your combo of choice (Alliteration and Consonance, or Alliteration and Assonance), and discover your verse. Don't set up your rhymes – let them come. It's amazing what happens when you just let it flow. Here's an example I just did, merely starting with the word "down" and not worrying at all about where the verse was going. All I had in my mind was the "DUM da da" cadence motif and knowing I was trying Alliteration and Consonance.

DUM da da
DOWN in the DEN there's a DIN and a SLAM
A gun, not again, for some gain there's a blam
The body of Betty, old biddy, went thwunk
He stuffs the old stiff in the back of the trunk.

Sondheim, eat your heart out! Cool, hunh? Who knew I had such a sick mind? That honestly came out spontaneously – not edited at all. It was easy, with the rhythm in my head and having practiced alliteration and assonance. I totally just said "thwunk" because it's what I heard in my head, and the "trunk" was just THERE!

Pick a cadence motif rhythm. You can start with DUM da da, since it's in your brain right now, and start going.

Do Exercise 62 now.

Repetition

Repetition is natural to do. Repetition is easy. Repetition highlights a word or phrase and makes it important. Orators do it a lot. Think of Dr. Martin Luther King's "I Have a Dream" speech, which uses that phrase over and over.

Songs naturally have repetition in them, because the title is repeated. And what we've been practicing (alliteration, consonance, assonance) is repetition of sounds. I'm talking here of repeating words and phrases (other than the title) within the song. But please use discipline. It takes very little to go from an interesting, intriguing repeating phrase that drives the lyric, to one that's too much and becomes boring.

Chiasmus

This one's mainly for songwriters, for when you have time to think and write. It's very hard to improvise, but wonderful to the ear! Chiasmus [ky-AZ-mus] is when the order of words in the first clause is switched around in the second clause. In the past, chiasmus referred to reordering the grammar, but is more popularly known now for reordering the words themselves. Here are some some examples of chiastic quotations:

> It's not the men in your life that counts, it's the life in your men.
> - Mae West in *I'm No Angel* (1933)

> One should eat to live, not live to eat.
> - (first attributed to) Socrates

> By failing to prepare, you are preparing to fail.
> - Benjamin Franklin

> When the going gets tough, the tough get going!
> - Anonymous

> ...ask not what your country can do for you - ask what you can do for your country
> - John F. Kennedy, *Inaugural Address*, January 20, 1961

> I'd rather have a bottle in front of me than a frontal lobotomy.
> - Tom Waits, on *Fernwood2night*, 1977 (origin not certain)

There is such balance using phrases like this. They are very pleasurable to listen to and make a strong impact on the listener.

Now Put It to Use!

Great writers - of song, speech, poetry, etc. - really do use these lyric devices throughout their work. Here are some examples of all the things we've been talking about by some word masters. See if you can spot all the instances of rhyme, alliteration, sibilance, consonance, and assonance. (The first one I'll mark for you!)

> The *s*ilken *s*ad *unc*ertain ru*s*tling of each **p**ur**p**le **c**ur*tain*
> - Edgar Allen Poe, *The Raven*, 1845

Boiling black clouds roiling in from the west
Clashing claps of thunder sent to steal my rest
> - Marshall Stern , "Peace,", 1994

Into the snows she sweeps,
Hurling the haven behind,
The Deutschland, on Sunday; and so the sky keeps,
For the infinite air is unkind,
And the sea flint-flake, black-backed in the regular blow,
Sitting Eastnortheast, in cursed quarter, the wind;
Wiry and white-fiery and whirlwind-swivelled snow
Spins to the widow-making unshilding unfathering deeps.
> - Gerald Manley Hopkins, *The Wreck of the Deutschland*, 1875

♪ ♪ ♪

Chapter 14
Figurative Language
Lyrics 401

Figurative Language

Figurative language creates figures, or pictures, so the listener or reader quickly gets a more vivid image and usually a deeper emotional understanding of what the artist is trying to convey.

When people first start improvising songs, they tend to gush out as many words as possible to explain what's going on, to set up a joke, to get to a rhyme word or whatever.

It's like newbie improvisers who must fill in any silence with speaking during a scene. As we get more comfortable and experienced on stage, we learn to use the silence and are able to use more or less words, as the character dictates.

Someone who is comfortable and experienced improvising songs doesn't have to fill in all the beats and have what equates with "verbal diarrhea." If you are using my method of fitting the cadence to the motif, you already will have lyrics that at the very least are broken into phrases, rather than just long lines all sounding the same.

As the Tao Te Ching says, "More words count less." Which is great advice for songwriters!

Figurative lyrics are shortcuts, since they paint emotional pictures for listeners. If I wanted you to understand my relationship with Marshall, I could sing lines and lines explaining how I feel a deep connection with him, one which makes me feel safe and peaceful, like I'm Home, yet joyful like a little kid, etc., etc. Or I can use imagery to describe the relationship, like "Warm, fresh-baked cookies closeness."

Most people get a warm, fuzzy, homey feeling when thinking about this image, and probably an excited feeling, from when they were kids and a parent made a batch of cookies! The point is, with a few words I get across not only what I want you to understand about my situation, but get you to feel it, too! Awesome!

With a little bit of practice, you can use more poetic, advanced lyrics. Just as with rhyming, the more you do it, the better you get at it.

Similes and metaphors are the biggies in figurative language, and they're very similar. If you get them mixed up, here's how I remember them...

A simile uses as or like. A metaphor doesn't.

Similes

Similes make comparisons between two things, using the words "as" or "like." That's it. So simple! In fact, musicians don't just use similes in their songs, but also in their titles. There's "**Like** a Rolling Stone" (Bob Dylan), "Thick **as** a Brick" (Jethro Tull), "Feel **Like** a Number" (Bob Seger), "Cold **as** Ice" (Foreigner), and "Smells **Like** Teen Spirit" (Nirvana).

And you know it's good when the Bard himself uses the device:

> Her beauty hangs upon the cheek of night,
> **Like** a rich jewel in an Ethiop's ear"
> *- Shakespeare, Romeo and Juliet, 1597*

Here are some more simile expressions that have been used so much that now they're cliché.

> As old as the hills
>
> As strong as a bull
>
> Drink like a fish
>
> Fight like cat and dogs

Try to stay away from clichés if you can. They are called cliché because so many people use them and are thus overused. Why would you want your song to be the same as so many others? It's much better to have fresh, new ideas and lyrics. Clichés *are* encouraged if you can use them in an entirely new way and context which gives original meaning to these old, familiar sayings. Or, of course, if your song is *about* clichés or worn ideas!

Exercise 63 - Rhythmic Similes

I'm going to have you do this in rhythm, which helps most people, since it's often harder to come up with something when there are too many possibilities. We'll narrow it a bit by doing it in a "da DUM da da DUM da da DUM(da)" rhythm. The stressed DUMs are the blanks you can fill in for the following statement:

> The _____ is as_____ as a _____.

Just look around you and pick a (one syllable) object. Then give it a descriptive word for the second blank, and then pick something else for the third blank that also could be described with that second word. For example:

> The COUCH is as TAN as a TOURist.

Hey. It doesn't have to make sense. If you're writing and editing, then worry about making sense later. Get it out of your brain right now.

> ∿∿∿∿∿∿
>
> For writers: My friends Andy Eninger and Steve Ma-
> tuszak (and the rest of the Chicago Comedy Com-
> pany gang, me included!) used to train companies
> on brainstorming. The problem often comes be-
> cause we combine the two processes of creating
> and editing. When we do that, we start getting
> ideas and then edit them before they're fully
> formed. ("No, that would never work..." "No, it
> sounds wrong...") This psyches you out, shuts you
> down, and your ideas come slower and slower.
> Whereas if you get all the ideas down on paper first,
> THEN go back and trash/edit/improve it, your
> brainstorming/writing usually will be much more
> prolific and profitable!
>
> ∿∿∿∿∿∿

You can replace some of the syllables if you want, for example:

The COUCH is **as** TAN **as** John BOEHner

But you DO have to say "is **as** _____ **as**" or "is da DUM **like** da DUM [da]"

The COUCH is eCRU **like** John BOEHner

Do Exercise 63 now.

Exercise 64 - Setting up Rhymed Similes

To set up a rhyme in a simile, you have to think a little back-wards. Just like thinking of the landing word first and then setting it up for the first line is thinking/rhyming backwards.

Let's start with forward rhyming, which still takes some backwards thinking! Do a line just like we did in the previous exercise – "the _____ is as _____ as a _____." For example, "The bed is as soft as a feather." Now you have to think of a rhyme for "feather," like, say, "weather." Next think of a descriptive word, and then another thing that also fits that description. But say that other thing FIRST. So it would be…

> The bed is as soft as a feather
> Your mood is as changeable as the weather.

Yes, I know the second line doesn't fit the rhythm, but that's okay. If you can have a consistent rhythm, that's great! If not, don't sweat it. This exercise is more about practicing similes. Practicing rhythms is a bonus!

When you get really good at this, try setting up your rhyme while setting up the similes. Meaning, think of your landing word first (you might now quickly pick the descriptive word and what else is like that, like we just did. This is your second line. Or you may wait until after you sing the first line to think of this.) Then you think of your setup rhyme word, its descriptive word and thing sharing that description for the FIRST line.

It's exactly what we did for the first part of this exercise, but we don't SAY the line we think of first, we keep it for the second line. So if I know I want to end on the word "Kiwi" (and who doesn't?!), I think "Kiwi," then come up with a rhyme (wee wee), a descriptive word (wet), and another thing that is wet (your ideas). So I would say…

> You ideas are all wet just like wee wee.
> Your nose is all hairy like kiwi!

(Sorry about the insulting nature of these similes. Your ideas are fantastic, and your nose isn't really that hairy.)

Personally, I didn't think of the entire second line first, just the landing word. (I knew that I would forget it anyway, so I waited until the first line was sung and then quickly said in my mind, " A Kiwi is what? Hairy. What else is hairy? Your nose! Ah, Your nose is all hairy like kiwi!")

Do Exercise 64 now.

Exercises 65 – Singing Similes

Now that you can speak similes in rhythm, you can easily put them to music! Play either one-verse or two-verse musical tracks and sing the last exercise. Start with forward rhyming, and once you get comfortable with that, move to setting up your rhymes. It's probably not going to make much cohesive sense, but it's great practice to come up with simile after simile.

Play TRACKS 11-15 and 41-44 (Sondheim) for one verse of practice, 18-22 and 45-46 (Sondheim) for two or more verses and do Exercise 65 now.

Metaphors

Knowing similes really helps you learn metaphors. As I said before, the metaphor doesn't use the words "as" or "like" to compare two things. It says it IS the other thing. For example:

All the world's a stage, and all the men and women merely players.
- William Shakespeare, *As You Like It*, 1623

All our words are but crumbs that fall down from the feast of the mind.
- Khalil Gibran, *Sand and Foam*, 1926

Shakespeare doesn't say that the world is LIKE a stage, and that men and women are LIKE players, he says it IS a stage and they ARE players. Gibran doesn't say our words are LIKE crumbs, but that they ARE crumbs.

Some songs which use metaphor are Pat Benatar's "Love is a Battlefield," Kansas' "Dust in the Wind," and USA for Africa's "We Are the World."

In the above exercise example, I could turn the simile into a metaphor by saying

Your ideas are wee-wee. / Your nose is a kiwi.

Very poetic!

Exercise 66 – Practicing Metaphors

Don't worry about rhythm for now. Start like we did with the similes – pick out an object in the room where you are. Get an emotional reaction to it. For example, there is a fan in my room. My emotional reaction to it is negative – it's loud and annoying. So I start the same as I did with the simile exercise – "the fan is..." then I say to myself, "loud and annoying like..." and then fill in that blank, but out loud "a riot. A mob pounding me on my head." So what people hear is "The fan is a riot. A mob pounding on my head."

As you practice, that pause where you are saying " [description] like" will get faster and faster.

The door is [hopeful, like]
sunshine beaming through puffy white clouds.

The tree is [constant and wonderful, like]
a sentinel, a friend, and a mother.

> ෴෴෴
>
> The emotional connection is vital, because if you feel something, you are more likely to have an emotional memory so you can more quickly associate your thing with another thing. I would not have thought to call a tree a "mother," if I was stuck in my head trying to think of clever words. But the feeling I had when looking at the tree was tender and strong – a similar feeling I get with the idea of motherhood.
>
> ෴෴෴

Do Exercise 66 now, for many objects/concepts.

Exercise 67 – Metaphors in Rhythm

We'll put a slow beat to this. Snap/clap/tap to a one one thousand, two one thousand, three one thousand, four one thousand beat.

Look around you and pick out an object. We'll discover a metaphor for it, but in rhythm.

My <u>DESK</u> is [<u>MESS</u>-y like] a <u>DRUNK</u>-en <u>FRAT</u> boy

The underlined syllables are the beats of the line. "Messy like" is NOT said out loud, so there are rests in the line. Try this with many objects around you.

Do Exercise 67 now.

Exercise 68 – Metaphors in Rhythm and Rhyme

Okay, the next step is to put these to rhyme. Let's just do forward rhyming. Start like you did for the last exercise – pick out an object and, to a fairly slow beat of four, say a metaphorical line in rhythm to the beat. Rest for the next four beats. Then start the next line with the same object and description. (The description is in your mind only, not said out loud.) It's an **abcb** rhyme scheme, so the last line will rhyme with line two.

For example,

> My desk is [messy like] a drunken frat boy
> [rest] [rest] [rest] [rest]
> My desk is [messy like] a drawn-out divorce.
> [rest] [rest] [rest] [rest]
> My desk is [messy like] a bratty child
> [rest] [rest] [rest] [rest]
> My desk is [messy like] a hurricane force.
> [rest] [rest] [rest] [rest]

If that's no problem, then get rid of the four beats in between each spoken line.

Do Exercise 68 now.

Exercise 69 – Singing Metaphors

As always, the next step is putting our new skill to music. This keeps us honest, because it's harder to cheat with the rhythm when there's actual music playing. Be aware of the beats and where lines begin and end. Play the tracks and sing the last exercise to music. Use a full line of music for one metaphor. If you get good at doing this, change the object as often as you wish.

I personally think that setting up metaphor rhymes is REALLY hard, so I'm not going to push you to do that. Although I encourage you to try it if you have the desire!

Play TRACKS 18-22 and 45-49 and do Exercise 69 now.

Yay!

Now you can practice all you want, using these fabulously advanced melodic and lyrical skills! Sing (and compose) verses and whole songs with the pleasing lyrical sounds we learned in Chapter 13, and the figurative lyrical devices we learned in Chapter 14.

Play TRACKS 11-15 and 41-44 (Sondheim) for one verse of practice, 18-22 and 45-46 (Sondheim) for two or more verses, and then 25-29 and 47 for Tagline full songs, 35-39 for Verse Chorus full songs, 47-49 for full Sondheim style songs, and practice, practice, practice!

♪ ♪ ♪

Chapter 15
Harmony 401

Ah, how wonderful when improvisers sing together and can harmonize! It makes the song seem, um…real. And if you can sing on pitch, you can harmonize!

First, a gentle caution. Just because you can harmonize, doesn't mean you always should. It's like a bass player that goes nuts, noodling around ALL the time. It's like an improviser in a scene who always takes focus, and talks whenever he is on stage. Or more appropriately, an improviser who always enters the scene. You certainly CAN enter every scene, but is it always the best thing for the scene? Same thing for the song. All the skills in this book should be used when the time is right. You wouldn't want to have alliteration in EVERY line you sing, and you don't need to harmonize constantly. (This coming from someone who LOVES to harmonize!) Harmony highlights sections of a song. If it's ALL highlighted, then it's as if NOTHING is highlighted.

Since you're spontaneously composing and singing these songs (unless you're writing and editing, in which case, ignore this point,) sometimes you'll want to harmonize and another singer will take the note that you're on. No worries, you can move to a different note! (Of course, what sometimes happens is that you both move to the same note, and then try moving back at the same time – just like when you're walking towards/past someone and you both move to the same side and block each other, then you both move to the other side, and back and forth, doing a little dance. I love when that happens!)

If you can hear the notes in a chord, you can harmonize. Simply pick a note in the chord being played, other than the one being sung by the main singer.

> ∾∾∾∾∾∾
>
> This is a great time to remind you that when you are singing, you should maintain awareness. Don't tune out the rest of the world! Many improvisers start talking or singing, and because they have focus, think that the world begins and ends with what they are doing. That doesn't make for good improv. When you're on stage, you want to sing loudly enough that you are heard by your fellow improvisers and audience, but softly enough that you can hear the music and any other singers. A good singer blends well with other voices, and you can't blend if you have little awareness and/or are singing at the top of your lungs. So it's good to practice a little volume restraint, especially in these next exercises.
>
> ∾∾∾∾∾∾

Exercise 70 – Hearing and Singing Notes in a Chord

Let's first practice hearing the notes in a chord. Track 51 will play various chords. At first, the individual notes that make up the chord will play, so you can hear them clearly, and then the full chord will be played many times in a short long, short long, short long rhythm. Each time the chord plays the long beat, jump to another note in the chord.

I'll play notes in the chord on the left hand as well at first, so sing along with those notes. But then the left hand will drop out. Continue jumping to different notes in the chord for each long beat. I'll switch to another chord and you'll sing all the notes in that new chord. I'll eventually stop playing the individual notes first and stop playing the left hand notes, and just play the chord itself. Like you did before, sing a different note in the chord for each long beat.

Play TRACK 51 and do Exercise 70 now.

Exercise 71 – More Advanced Harmony Exercise

I'll play a melody, over eight beats, three times. Listen to the first one, and then either sing along with it the second time and harmonize on the third, or if you can, harmonize on the second time, and do a different harmony on the third time. The accompaniment chord will change for each melody. Extra credit: find where my cat meows once during this exercise!

Play TRACK 52 and do Exercise 71 now.

Exercise 72 - Marshall's Good Harmony Song

Track 53 is a song Marshall Stern wrote (called "Song of the Angels") – it doesn't have words, so you don't have to worry about that as you sing along. Simply harmonize with what Marshall is singing. You can play this track many times and find different ways to harmonize. Every time I hear this, I MUST sing along to his soaring melody with my own harmony!

Play TRACK 53 and do Exercise 72 now.

Exercise 73 - Harmonize on Your Own

If you have a way to record at home (phone, computer, etc.), you can practice harmonizing to your heart's content! Record yourself singing to any of the musical tracks in this book, and when you play it back, harmonize to it. The chorus tracks are especially helpful for this.

Start without words, and then as you get better, record yourself singing regular songs with words.

This is not only great harmony practice, but it will show you areas where you need help. If you're singing too much on one note, the harmony will most likely match the boring nature of your melody! Are your words so fast and furious, or your notes not definite enough (you slide around on your notes, or don't really hit any notes right on key) that it's hard to harmonize with? If you find it difficult, probably others will, too. Notice if it's easy or difficult to harmonize with your songs, paying particular attention to your choruses.

Record yourself (especially using TRACKS 30-34) and harmonize when playing it back, to do Exercise 73 now.

Of course, you can practice harmonizing whenever you listen to music. I've always loved harmonizing. I sang alto in choruses ALL through school, was in the Swinging 'Gates - an a cappella group in college - and I still sing harmony in caroling groups to this day. When I sing along to music, I rarely take the melody line. Practice singing along with songs you know, but sing notes in the chords that are different from the melody notes. As with everything, the more you practice, the better you get!

♪ ♪ ♪

Chapter 16
Group Singing and Long-Form Improvised Musicals

Since improvised songs are brand new and never before heard, you may think it's impossible to sing with two or more people. Wrong-o! There are many ways for groups to sing together.

The Mind Meld Method

This is not a favorite of mine, but can be very funny if done well. It's what you do in church or temple when you don't know the words of the hymn. You sing along, and try your best to act like you DO know the words. It's like a vocal mirror exercise (you know, the mirror exercise where two people face each other, one keeps moving, and the other person mirrors the leader, trying to move exactly in unison with him/her.)

So with this, two or more singers sing the same exact words at the same exact time, either with one person leading, or switching the lead back and forth. It tends to be messy, but can be funny.

People use this method to a small degree in the rap/hip-hop style, where the singer sets up a landing word and everyone sings/says that word all together at the end of the line.

Echo/Respond

Musically, this is an easy way for people to join a song. When the main singer pauses, during the rests, other singers can echo the word or phrase just sung. (i.e. Main singer, "That's why I love my kiwi fruit!" Others echo, "my kiwi fruit!") Or I often see improvisers who are going for laughs respond to or comment on what the main singer has just said. (i.e. Main singer, "That's why I love my kiwi fruit!" Second singer, "and it looks like a testicle!")

Use this judiciously, though. It gets really tiring when overused. Yes, we get that you're echoing EVERY line! Yes, we get that you're really funny with comments during EVERY pause! Give your audience a break and use this when you really need it – not all the time.

Harmony

Harmonizing is another way to sing together during an improvised song. One pet peeve of mine is that people try harmonizing lyrics when they're not sure of the words, so it comes out as a messy jumble. What I suggest is to "oooh" behind the main singer, until you get to lyrics you know. (Which means you really have to know song formats!)

Counterpoint Melody (Countermelody) and Descants

These are almost a combination of echoing and harmonizing. That's because they sound different and move independently from the melody line, yet when put together with the melody, they create lovely harmony. Think of descants and countermelodies as ornamental melodies sung above or below the true melody. These lines don't merely echo the exact melody line on higher notes– they're independent! You've heard countermelodies and descants – gospel songs use them (often improvised!) a lot.

On Track 54, in the familiar piece "Stars and Stripes Forever" you can hear the melody line, the piccolos playing the descant high above everything, and the trombones playing a countermelody.

Play TRACK 54 to hear an excerpt of "Stars and Stripes Forever" now.

The Importance of Using Song Formats and Song Titles

If you know what song format you're using, it's MUCH easier to sing as a cohesive and professional sounding group. And to know what format you're in (unless you've decided ahead of time), you NEED to TITLE YOUR SONG!!

TITLE YOUR SONG!!

I can't stress this enough. For some reason, improvisers think it's cheating to title their songs, or they forget, or they do and then forget and end up changing the title, or they just plain don't want to. So they end up discovering the title while they are singing. That can be absolutely fine for a solo song or for a more free-form song, like in the style of Sondheim. But if you wait to title it until you're actually singing, I've noticed common problems.

1. It often takes longer to get around to the title.
2. If the title is where it's supposed to be (and gotten to quickly), it often doesn't make the most sense, since it was just there because it rhymed with the line before.
3. The singer thinks s/he sang the title, but the musician doesn't recognize it as such, and they are on different pages to where in the song they think they are!

4. The song is just generally messier, since people think different things are needed and are going their own way. Too many cooks, as it were.

If you title your song before singing and stick to song formats, then everyone knows where you are in the song, and can support you in it.

Before every show of *MUSICAL! the musical,* I would have the actors do a three-line offer/accept scene into song. The third line was the song title, and would have to be said in a very obvious and over-the-top "This is the song title!" way. Then the musician would play, since the actor was clearly calling for a song. Whoever titled the song would sing the first verse. If the title was said in the first or last line of that verse, everybody (including the musician) knew that it was a Tagline song. The musician would play another verse, which the second person in that scene would sing, putting the title in the same place in that verse. If the verse did NOT have the title in it, then everybody knew that it was a Verse Chorus song. The musician would go into a chorus, and the second person would sing a catchy chorus with the title in it. (If the musician decided to play a very Sondheimian-sounding accompaniment, we knew it was Sondheim-style.)

Having a title and a sticking to a song format makes your made-up song seem real and written, which is very important if you want a professional slick show. It also allows your fellow players to support you rather than guessing at what you might want or need.

Duets and Trios

It's important to remember that the musician plays the same chord progression in a song every time s/he plays the verse or the chorus (or bridge, if the bridge is played more than once.) If you know this, then you can do some fun things to sing together!

A Chorus is the most obvious case of the musician playing the same chord progression, since the singer sings (or TRYS to sing!) the exact same thing that was originally sung for the first chorus. You KNOW it's going to be repeated. So you and your entire group can harmonize and fill in with countermelodies and descants.

When I was in ImprovBoston, we would do a Tagline duet song, where Person 1 would sing the first verse, Person 2 would sing the second verse, they would split the bridge, and then one would take the lead on the final verse, with the other harmonizing, echoing, and doing descants. Fun.

We upped the bar in *MUSICAL! the musical*. Our standard format for what we call the Love Duet is:

× VERSE 1 - Person 1 would sing the first verse as a last line Tagline (The last line being the title.)

× VERSE 2 - Person 2 would sing the second verse, but with a completely different countermelody (Of course, ending with the title.)

× BRIDGE

  Line 1 - Person 1 would set up Person 2 for a landing word.
  Line 2 - Person 2 would try to end on that landing word.
  Line 3 - Person 2 would set up a landing word.
  Line 4 - Person 1 would try to end on the landing word.

× VERSE 3 - Person 1 and 2 sing their exact previous verse (or as exact as possible). If done well, the melodies contrast with each other and yet harmonize really well.

× Nice harmony on the final line/ending of song.

You can find an example of *MUSICAL! the musical*'s Love Duet on YouTube – search "Musical! Love Duet Instant Songwriting" and it should be the first (non-promoted) video listed. I'm also posting various improvised songs under my name –NancyHowlandWalker – feel free to subscribe to my channel!

Once you understand that anything sung to a certain chord progression can go with something different sung to that same chord progression, you can have tons of fun. The Love Duet was one way we played with this idea. We also did trios.

With trios, we often did Verse songs, although we sometimes would go into Bridges. We either did just straight Verses with the title in the last line, or each character would do a monologue and then sing his/her verse. Right after the third verse, all three characters would sing their verse together. Again, you can see and hear an example on YouTube.

You can do this with any musical section which is the same. I've been talking about verses, but you could try it with choruses as well. For example, a character sings a catchy chorus with the title in it. The next time the chorus comes back, an opposing character could sing a contrasting chorus, still using that title. The third time the chorus comes back, the two characters sing their own chorus at the same time. The end of the song would probably be the title repeated a couple of times.

One way to remember your verse or chorus while the next person is singing theirs, is to sing yours in your head during the other verses or choruses, until you all have to sing together.

Some people are naturals when it comes to singing a counter-melody, and others have a lot of trouble. I think you have a leg up if you've been in bands/orchestras/choral groups, because then you're used to hearing countermelodies. Some things to help you...

1. Contrast the timing of when you sing. Be aware of when the first person's lines begin and end. If they are standard lines which start on beat 1 and go to the 5th or 7th beat, then you may want do a pick up to each line (start singing before beat 1) in order to fill that pause. Besides pick up notes, another easy way to do this is to note what rhyme scheme the first person is using, and contrast that. Most people do an **aabb** rhyme scheme. If you did something different, say an **a (bb) a (cc)** rhyme scheme (where "**bb**" and "**cc**" are internal rhymes), then you'll pause at different points, filling in spaces not normally filled in by others.

2.Contrast the speed. If the first person is singing rather wordy, fast lyrics, you can slow down and do very few and slow lyrics.

3.Contrast the pitch/tone. Sing like a musical instrument. Choose one and sing like that instrument would sound. If you're singing like a tuba, and someone else sings like a violin, and another sings like a piccolo, each verse will sound very different, yet probably work very well together!

Exercise 74 – Sing like an Instrument

Play Tracks 18-22 which have two verses in a row. Pick a song title, and sing the first verse (with words - last line tagline) as a particular instrument. Sing the next verse as a completely different instrument, trying to contrast and complement your melody from the first verse. Try it again, singing one verse quickly, and one slowly. If you have any way of recording yourself, record your 1st verse, sing the 2nd verse, and then immediately play back the first verse and sing your 2nd verse over the 1st. How does it sound? Do they complement each other? The rhythm and the notes should be different enough to sound really good when sung together.

Play TRACKS 18-22 and do Exercise 74 now.

Long-Form Improvised Musicals

In 1998, I created a fabulous show called *MUSICAL! the musical,* which was the United States' first two-act completely improvised narrative Broadway-style musical. We took a suggestion of an actual story and turned it into a 90-120 minute Broadway musical. The show garnered amazingly positive reviews from every paper in the Chicago area. We've done nearly one thousand absolutely original shows. So I know whereof I speak, when it comes to long-form improvised musicals. I could write an entire book on this topic. (Maybe I will!)

Suffice it to say, there are things that make long-form musicals more professional and much better to watch. A lot of it comes down to VARIETY.

Variety in Song Style and Type

Songs should be distinct from one another. You don't have to go all Joseph and the Amazing Technicolor Dreamcoat on your audience and go down a checklist of different song styles, but your songs should have different flavors, which give them different energies.

Song Formats

Use different song formats. If all your songs are Verse Chorus or your group always sings Tagline songs, it will get boring to your audience's ear. They will know that a chorus is coming up, they will expect it, and so when it comes, it's not as pleasurable as it could be. Because the emotional levels are different for the various song formats, using a good mix will add variety to the show.

Song Types

There are different typical types of songs in a musical, which tend to have their own flavor. Some improv groups get stuck using one or two (often the "I Am" type of song which are mostly expositions about - surprise! - who an individual or group is and what the situation is), making the energy and songs all one level. Each type of song has a certain energy and quality which brings variety to the show. The opening number should set the mood and tone of the show to come. In *MUSICAL!*, we were spoofing the very serious, angsty Broadway-style musical, so our opening number usually had a tense and driving feel. There's the "I Wish" or "I Want" song, which tells what a character truly wants. (An objective! Imperative in any narrative!) There are the "I Am/We Are" songs that I mentioned above. There are "Love Songs," which can be solo or duets or more, depending on the kind of love! Oh, heck, here's a partial list of various types of songs in a musical. You can probably think of one or two examples for most of these.

× Opening Number

× I Wish/I Want

× I Am/We Are

× Love Song

× Eleven O'clock Song

× Finale Song

× Angry Mob Song

× Crowd Song (often a "We Are" song)

× Dying/Death/Grief Song

× Minor Character/Sidekick Song

× Singing About Your Work/Chores Song

× Story/Parable Song

× Villain Song

× Voyaging/Want to Travel Song

× Inspiring March-type Song

× Multi-Main-Character Huge Something's About to Happen (can contain Reprises) Song

× Song Before the Storm

× Reprises

Dynamics

When I go to a musical improv show, or watch some on You-Tube, I'm always struck by how much everyone practically screams their songs. I don't know why so many improvisers feel the need to sing as loudly as possible every single second of every single song. Or if they DO soften up for a love song, for example, that song is still all at one volume level. I know it's hard when you're making it up, but with solos especially, the musician and the singer should be able to lead and follow each other and grow louder and softer together. As groups get used to singing together, they absolutely can all get soft or loud together. It's a matter of practice.

Number of People Singing

When I lived in Boston, a woman once hired me to consult on a musical she was writing. It was a fine musical, with the exception that every one of her songs was a solo. Improv groups often have the opposite problem, with every song being a group number. (People jumping in to add harmony or singing to Taglines/Choruses simply because they know the words or that they can.) Please vary the number of people singing each song, as that varies the energy, which is good!

Even in a two-person long-form musical, you do NOT need both people singing each song. Have solos and duets, and if your musician is up to singing, have that voice added for harmony occasionally. It makes for a much more enjoyable experience.

Song Endings

Try to vary how you end your songs. You WILL need to practice this as a group, because it's very easy to get stuck in one type of ending. Please, for the love of God, don't end EVERY song with a major ritard. I know it's tempting to slow down and Alllllllll Siiii-innngggggg Tooooooo-geeeeeeehthhhhhhh-eeeeeeeeeeeeeeeeeeeeeeeeeeeeeer! But it will really drag down the energy of your show. Here are some possible ways to end your improv songs:

- Slow Down or Speed Up
- Get Loud or Soft
- Sudden, Short Ending
- Long Note
- Tag - Repeat Last Line/Title
- Button - Song ends and one Character makes funny (sung or spoken) comment or Sound Effect
- End Singing, Musician Outros the Song
- Repeat and Fade
- Song Interrupted (i.e. by a scream or character entering with some news)
- Final Note Sung High and Long (Great for solos, or in a group, let the main character sing that note all alone)
- End Big and Strike a Big Pose (i.e. 1 or 2 arms up)

A strong ending is very important because it lets the audience know the song's over and that they should applaud. There is nothing worse than singing an improv song, and afterwards the audience is silent, or gives tepid, uncertain applause. This goes for songs in short-form AND long-form shows. I've done the same musical game (Bartender) with different musicians, where one accompanist will listen to the singer and end the song strongly, and the other just sort of peters out after each song. The game always goes so well for the first musician and has a weird energy for the second. Why? Because people knew when to applaud with the first guy, and because they clapped, they thought they liked the entire game better than the audience who didn't applaud during the game at all. Also, the musical button, which the first musician inevitably gave, made the lyrical joke seem funnier (like an old time rim shot.)

For a strong group-song ending, the improvisers must be on the same page with each other AND the musician. That's why it's a good idea to have a leader standing the most downstage to lead the ending. Whoever originally sang the chorus should be in charge of it and the ending. (If it's a Verse Chorus song, you are most likely ending on the Chorus.) The leader can indicate physically if there's a change in dynamics. Very naturally, if the leader physically contracts, you know that the volume is decreasing. If s/he expands physically, it's a good bet the volume is going to get loud! Or s/he might want you to stop singing and give a subtle (or not-so subtle) "stop singing" gesture. Of course, the leader can cut everybody off at the same time at the very end of the song. (If the musician is in everyone's sightline, s/he can lead the end as well.)

The leader/singer should feel free to get eye contact with the musician. Why make it harder on yourself by just using your ears? If you can see each other fairly easily, then communicate with a look! I often think that musicians must be very lonely during improv shows, since the actors hardly ever look at them, even when it would be very helpful to do so!

The Nonmusical Part of the Show

The variety you put in your songs should also be used in the nonmusical improvised scenes. This goes for regular improv shows as well. Each scene should vary from each other and within itself regarding dynamics, energy, number of people on stage, activity, and level of seriousness. I personally get really tired at shows where every scene has two people standing and talking, trying to be as loud, funny and wacky as possible. There is no variety, and therefore no flow, no tension and release. No maturity.

Whereas an improviser who can't really sing well can do great short-form musical numbers by selling the style, emotion and energy of the song, it can get tiring in a long-form musical to hear bad singers. For a full-length show, I do recommend casting improvisers who can carry a pitch, harmonize and have enough musical knowledge to vary what and how they sing.

Wheee!

Long-form musical improv can be an incredibly artistically rewarding endeavor. *MUSICAL! the musical* was a wonderful experience, and I still hear from former cast mates how important and/or fulfilling it was to them! As this book goes to print, a UK based group (The Maydays) is rehearsing for a run of *MUSICAL! the musical*, and I hope it's as artistically satisfying to them as it was on this side of the pond!

Afterword

Musical Improv is such a new art form, which has exploded over the last 10-15 years. In the year 2000, there were only a handful of groups dedicated to musical improv in only a few countries. Now there are a number of groups in most cities around the globe! There's even a New York Musical Improv Festival every year in the autumn. How fantastic is that?!

I've been so fortunate to have created and taught courses in musical improv since 1995 (and individual classes before that), so I've seen the leaps and bounds that this art form has taken. And it IS astounding how far it has come and what is still possible.

I hope I've given beginner improvisers the confidence and knowledge to create songs on the spot. I hope that I've given new skills and goals to those who are already experienced in musical improv.

And I hope that songwriters can use these skills and techniques to free up the flow and discover the genius lyrics and songs just waiting to burst forth.

You want your musical improv, whether one game in a short-form show or a full improvised musical, to be the best, most amazing experience for yourself and for the audience. You want them to leave saying, "Hot Dang, that was amazing! How did they DO it?!" You want your songs, written or improvised, to speak to your listeners and mean something to them.

The website for this book is a place for musical improvisers (Dunce to Diva!) and songwriters to engage, discuss and continue learning about this art form. Please go to www.InstantSongwriting.com and leave questions, comments, and use whatever tools and information we have. If you'd find something helpful, please let me know, and I'll try to get it on the website!

For all, Dunce to Diva, I say, "Give voice to the song in your heart!" We connect with our joyous, true nature when we do!

About the Author

NANCY HOWLAND WALKER is a full time SAG/AFTRA actor, writer, teacher and trainer who has been performing, teaching, directing, and producing improv since 1989. In Boston, she was the Artistic Director of TheatreSports and ImprovBoston (New England's longest running professional comedy troupe). In Chicago, she is the Executive Director of Chicago Improv Associates, which offers improv-based entertainment and corporate training.

Nancy's specialty is musical improv. She has sung short-form musical improv games with ImprovBoston, the International Improvisational Theater League, TheatreSports, Just For Laughs, and the Disney Cruise Line. Nancy has also sung in long-form improvised musicals with ImprovBoston and the Free Associates (*Divamatic,* an improvised cabaret), and in 1998, Nancy created, produced, directed and performed in the critically acclaimed show *MUSICAL! the musical,* the country's first two-act completely improvised modern Broadway style musical, which opened at Chicago's Royal George Theatre, and has had runs in Boston, Nashville and various theaters across the United States and now the United Kingdom. Nancy has developed one-day, weekend, and full eight-week musical improv curricula for improv schools, troupes and festivals, and has taught the subject to packed classes all over the world.

Connect to the Author

Website: www.InstantSongwriting.com
Email: Nancy@InstantSongwriting.com
FaceBook: Instant Songwriting Page (please Like!)
Twitter: @nhwsong
YouTube: Nancy Howland Walker channel (or search "zenprov")
for musical improv videos
Zenprov: search on iTunes for the podcast or go directly to
www.cia.libsyn.com, and twitter @zenprov

Nancy is available for hire, to teach workshops on musical improv, Zenprov , scenic improv, stage combat for improvisers, and a plethora of other improv related subjects. (She's been doing improv for a long time!)

Nancy, along with Marshall Stern, runs Chicago Improv Associates, which offers comedy entertainment and fun and effective corporate workshops in such areas as communication, leadership, team building, and creativity. If you would like to book her for corporate training or entertainment - improv, sketch, holiday caroling, etc. - email her at Nancy@ChicagoImprovAssociates.com.

Contributing
Musician Biographies

KRIS ANDERSON has performed in improvisational theatre since 1991. After enjoying improv as an audience member for years, Kris became the fifth member of ground-breaking Brisbane improv troupe Out on a Limb, performing mixed short and long-form shows. In 1992 he featured as the musician for Lightning Doubles, a Theatresports-branded improv show making its debut in the first annual Brisbane Comedy Bananza. While away from Australia during 1994-1995, Kris performed regularly with Denver's Headgames ensemble in Boulder, Colorado. Over the last two decades, Kris has featured with every major improv group in Brisbane, including ImproMafia, Theatresports, Out on a Limb, Impro Gladiators, EDGE Improv, and the improv comedy game show, Bite the Bucket. Kris teaches musical improv workshops, and accompanies hundreds of Brisbane high school kids each year in the annual Youth Theatresports Festival. In 2011 Kris shared the stage with the country's best at the 2011 Australian Theatresports National Championships. Kris writes and maintains Musical Hotspot (musicalhotspot.com), the most extensive resource on the internet for actors and musicians working in improvised theatre. Kris' other musical pursuits have included scoring short films, busking, and performing with originals and covers bands. Kris also publishes short improvised piano pieces at Uncomposed (uncomposedmusic.com).

JEFF BOUTHIETTE is currently head of the Music Program for Second City in Chicago. He has music directed for improv and sketch comedy extensively in the city of Chicago, including with the Second City National Tour and at sea, Comedysportz, The Comedy Shrine, Chicago Comedy Company, Gayco and others. As an improviser, he was a longtime member of the musical improv troupe Jazz Hands Across America, and currently performs with the Second City Training Center Music Improv House Ensemble, Infinite Sundaes. As an actor, Jeff has performed with Pegasus Players, Hell in a Handbag, Theatre Hikes, Brown Couch, Stage Two, Arts Lanes, One Theatre, and Chicago Kids Company. He played Montel/Jesus in Bailiwick Repertory's award-winning production of Jerry Springer: The Opera. As a theatrical musical director, Jeff has worked with Theatre Building Chicago, Lil' Buds Theatre, Stage Left, Victory Gardens Theatre, and Chicago Children's Theatre. In 2007, Jeff participated in the Johnny Mercer Songwriting Project as one of the nation's top young songwriters. Jeff is also Artistic Director of Bare Boned Theatre.

ROBBIE ELLIS is a New Zealand composer, performer, musician, human and being. Born in Auckland, he began performing improv theatre in 2001 while still in high school. He has worked extensively with ConArtists in Auckland; The Improvisors in Wellington; and Wellington Improvisation Troupe, primarily as a musician and occasionally as an actor. As of early 2012, he had co-created 77 improvised musicals, including seasons of Austen Found: The Undiscovered Musicals of Jane Austen (sold out, 2010 Adelaide Fringe Festival) and Improv: The Secondary School Musical (Best Comedy, 2009 New Zealand Fringe Festival). He has performed improv all around New Zealand, as well as in Melbourne, Adelaide and Rotterdam. For four years, Robbie worked as a producer and presenter for Radio New Zealand Concert, the fine music station of the national public broadcaster. He is also a composer who has had pieces performed by the New Zealand Symphony Orchestra and Auckland Philharmonia Orchestra. In January 2012, he moved to Dunedin to take up the University of Otago Mozart Fellowship in Composition. He plans to use his time to write a non-improvised musical. Website: www.robbie.co.nz

MIKE DESCOTEAUX is the director of the nationally renown Charles River Creative Arts Program in Boston, MA. He also directs ImprovBoston's touring company and is a resident musician there. Mike served as head of the Music Program at The Second City Training Center and music director of the Second City ETC stage in Chicago. He has had the privilege of working with Tony Award-winning artists such as Jason Robert Brown, William Finn, Mark Hollmann, and James LaPine. He has "composed" and "conducted" over 1,000 completely improvised musicals with Musical! The Musical, Baby Wants Candy (head music director), I Eat Pandas, Diva (director) and Jazz Hands Across America (artistic director). His original musicals include Sodomites!, Warfield, USA! The Fundamental Skip, The Magic Ofrenda, This Time, and Ready for Life: a zombie musical. He is the director/creator of the hit satire The Best Church of God and has been seen on NBC, CBS, A&E, and WGN. Mike, a Northwestern grad, has received a Jeff Award, After Dark Award, Paynter Award and was named one of the top young songwriters in the country by the Johnny Mercer/AMTP association. Mike is a member of ASCAP and the Boston Musicians' Association.

STEPHEN GILBANE has been accompanying improv troupes and teaching improvisers to make up songs on the spot since joining ImprovBoston in 1992, when the troupe (along with Ms. Walker, Adam Felber and others) developed their signature long-form improvised musical format. He was artistic director (1999-2005) of Musical Improv Company, an improvisational troupe that specialized in developing and performing full-length improvised musicals. More recently, he has composed music (and produced cast recordings) for eight of ImprovBoston's annual Halloween scripted musical Gorefest productions (including 2010's Cirque du Slaughté, available on iTunes). He has co-written several short musicals (including History Of Nails!, developed improvisationally), is creator of Showstopper! A High-Tech Musical (based on a startup company in the mid-1980's) and is composer for Pirate Lives (a full-length musical involving Noel Coward characters and pirates, having its planned world premiere in 2012). He attended Berklee College to study film scoring, and composed music for the horror film Bit Parts (Elftwin Films), as well as seven manic Boston 48-Hour Film Project films. Steve is a Java programmer by day to support his often-expensive music habit.

GEORGE GOETSCHEL began his piano playing in early childhood when he would improvise with his father on the accordion. He won first place in trumpet and piano in every competition he entered during his High School and College days. After his schooling at Governors State University, he toured throughout South America and Europe with world renowned musicians. He worked throughout the 70's and 80's with bands that shared the stage with Ramsey Lewis and was regularly appearing at such notable clubs as the Jazz Showcase. Mr. Goetschel's original compositions and improvisations have been featured in shows on NBC-TV and at the famed Improv, iO and Second City Theaters in Chicago. His solo piano compact disc release, "21 in the Moment" on the Emphasis Music label, received rave reviews from the press and public alike. He has since released two more compact discs, "Remembrances" and "Songs of Nature". Mr. Goetschel has also taught music and drama in the public and private schools for ten years. Currently he teaches music at Chicago Vocational High School in Chicago and teaches privately (piano and trumpet) in Evanston, IL.

RACHEL KAUFMAN is a multi-instrumentalist in NYC who has been playing for improv comedy groups since 1991, and has performed in an insane variety of venues, ranging from playing Gospel piano at a Baptist church in Chicago to playing trombone in the Labor Day Parade on Fifth Avenue. She has played either piano, accordion, or guitar for such groups as Chicago City Limits, The Improvo-holics, Comedy Sportz, 8-bar Cut, Off-Off Campus (at the Edinburgh Festival), Atomic Pile (directed by Urinetown composer Mark Holl-mann), Burn Manhattan, The Polyannas, The Unconnected.com (at Caroline's Comedy Club), and many others, as well as for numerous groups from all over the USA at the Funny Women Fest 2000 in Chicago. She has also music directed and/or played for well over 250 musicals and cabaret shows all over the world. Rachel can also be seen playing for auditions, classes, improv comedy groups, at restaurants, piano bars, and on cruise ships. She holds a B.A. in Music (and Russian) from the University of Chicago. Contact: radinishmini@yahoo.com

ART KOSHI has done accompanist work for the improvisational comedy group On The Spot (2006 to present), Ballet Hawaii (1996-present), The University of Hawaii Dance Department (2000 to present), & The Pacific Ballet Academy (1997-2000). His composition work includes the soundtrack for a UH Dance Department Senior Thesis Piece entitled: "Green Blanket Feet" (2010), the musical score for works in Cherry Blossom Cabaret's "Carnal Carnival" (2011), Femme Capulet (2011), a collaboration with takashi koshi on the soundtrack for the movie Modern Runaway (2011) and is currently composing music for Cherry Blossom Cabaret's "Last Chance Saloon" (2012). Art's relationship with improvising music began in the dance classroom. It was in this setting where he was taught that improvised music was better suited for the unpredictable nature of the class. Art's experience in playing for dance classes later led to an improvised musical collaboration with On The Spot. With On The Spot, Art has performed musically in improvisational theatre festivals such as Honolulu's Improvaganza (2007-2011), Austin's Out of Bounds (2009), The Phoenix Improv Festival (2010), The Chicago Improv Festival (2011), and The Seattle Improv Festival (2012). artkoshi@gmail.com
http://soundcloud.com/koshi-1

MICHAEL POLLOCK is in his 10th year as a musical director at The Second City Hollywood Training Center. He also works full-time on various shows at Disneyland and accompanies "Opening Night: The Improvised Musical" each week at IOWest. He is the author of Musical Improv Comedy, Musical Direction for Improv and Sketch Comedy and How to Write Funny Lyrics. His arranging credits include The Drew Carey Show, The Tonight Show, Evening at the Improv, and the Emmy Award-winning Tuesdays With Morrie. He wrote "Remember Tonight and Smile" for Columbia Pictures' Punchline, starring Tom Hanks and Sally Field, and orchestrated Universal Studios Hollywood's live Adventures of Rocky and Bullwinkle. He trained at the University of Texas at Austin, Pacific Conservatory of Performing Arts and the Grove School of Music. Special thanks to Chandler Coates, who engineered Michael's piano tracks for this book!

JAMEY ROSEN has been accompanying improvisational theatre, comedy, and spoken word for over 20 years. He has taught courses on improvised singing and improvised accompaniment at the Chicago, Seattle and Miami Improv Festivals and in colleges and theatre schools. Jamey lives in Ontario, Canada.

JOE SAMUEL is a classically trained pianist and violinist having studied music at Royal Holloway University of London. He has been a professional musician for 15 years, playing in a variety of successful bands on both his electric violin and on keyboard. He joined The Maydays in 2007 and is their Musical Director, performing regularly in London and Brighton. He is also the Musical Director of The Treason Show, BAFTA nominated sketch comedy show based in Brighton. Joe runs the website www.musicalimprovcomedy.co.uk with fellow improviser, Heather Urquhart, producing resources, podcasts and articles related to all things improvised and musical. He also tours the UK providing workshops, training and facilitation from improv troupes to management teams. Joe's interest in harmony and analysis has also led him to discovering a new way of teaching and understanding chords and harmony, and he now runs a project called SeeChord which helps students, teachers and songwriters hone their skills. SeeChord.co.uk is the hub of this project.

JEFFREY L SHIVAR has been a professional theater musician in Chicago, IL since 1988. He is currently a musician at ComedySportz Chicago, where he served as Musical Director from 1996-2005, and the Comedy Shrine of Aurora, IL. Mr. Shivar has performed music with every major improv group in Chicago, including The Second City Touring Companies, The Annoyance Theater, iO (formerly ImprovOlympic), Noble Fool Theater, and MUSICAL! the Musical. He has worked with children's theaters, including Emerald City Theater and Gaia Theater, as well as working with the Addison's Children's Theater from 1999-2004. As a composer, Mr. Shivar has created many scores for theatrical productions with WNEP Theater, including the musical The Wicked and the Sexed and Crosscurrents, a wordless play set to music. He has also written music for the aforementioned Addison's Children's Theater and ComedySportz's Family Series. Mr. Shivar attended the University of Cincinnati, where he studied music composition and theory at U.C.'s College Conservatory of Music. He earned a B.A. in Theater Arts from Wright State University.

FRANK SPITZNAGEL is a graduate of the Boston Conservatory of Music. His National Tours include Peter Pan, A Chorus Line, and Evita. He has played for and musical directed over 50 shows, from Annie to Zorba. Frank was also the musical director for the Chicago City Limits resident company for 9 years, then went on to play many improv classes and all the famous NYC Improv venues. His work has been seen on Comedy Central, in the Aspen Comedy Festival, and in Indie films. Frank is also the accompanist for the Lincoln Center "Meet the Artist" series. He has performed with Ithzak Perlman and scores of Broadway stars.

MARSHALL STERN has been a musician for 40 years, playing drums, bass, rhythm guitar and doing lead and background vocals at one time or another during that span. As a talented songwriter/musician, Marshall worked as a professional songwriter contracted by a subsidiary of Warner Chappel and many of Marshall 's songs appear on albums by Nashville recording artists and on other albums across the country and internationally. He is also a professional actor having appeared in many theatrical productions. Marshall has been performing and teaching improv since 1986 and has received many awards and honors in that field as well. Improv highlights include: receiving a Ruth Sweet Award for excellence in theatrical education, having his Improv troupe chosen to be the first to appear at the prestigious Humana Festival and being voted the best performing arts group in the Nashville Scene Readers poll. Marshall is a former director of The Players Workshop of The Second City. He sings with the Frozen Robins as well and has produced, directed, and performed in the Music City production of MUSICAL! the musical, where he was also the Artistic Director of One Hand Clapping. He is currently Artistic Director of Chicago Improv Associates and part of the duo that produces the Zenprov podcast.

LISA WEBB is originally from St. Louis, and has studied music in Missouri and Texas, receiving her Master's degree in Composition from North Texas State. A resident of Los Angeles for four years, she wrote and performed music, most notably with the LA Jazz Choir ~ a group which has performed and recorded with Rosemary Clooney, Steve Allen, Bob Hope and Linda Ronstadt among others. Since moving to Nashville, she has pursued a career as a musician and arranger and has songs cut in the U.S., Canada and Europe. She is involved in Artist production and special projects in Nashville, Chicago, Los Angeles and Miami. She also performs live in Nashville as well as numerous private and Corporate parties throughout the United States.

Appendix A

List of Exercises

1. Hearing the Emotion of the Music/Selling It!
2. Making up Different Melodies – Eight Beat Melody Lines

   2A. Five Beat Melody Lines

   2B. Various Melody Length Lines
3. Ear Training
4. Melodies in a Full Verse
5. Putting Words With Melody
6. Word Association
7. Rhyme Association
8. Easy Masculine Rhymes
9. Seemingly Harder Masculine Rhymes
10. Easier Feminine Rhymes
11. Seemingly Harder Feminine Rhymes
12. Word Melodies
13. Word Melodies to Verse Music

30B. Filling Various Beats

31. (A-E) Practicing Different Choruses

32. Entire Verse Chorus Songs

33. Single Sondheim Emotional Verses

34. Wordiness Warm-up

35. Double Sondheim Emotion Verses

36. Singing Lists

37. Musical Motifs

    37A. Simple Two Note Motif Exercise

    37B. Three and More Note Motifs

38. Musical Motifs to a Full Verse

39. Iambic Speaking

40. More Iambic Speaking

    40A. Iambic Speaking to Music

    40B. Forward Rhyming, Iambic Speaking to Music

    40C. Setting Up Rhymes, Iambic Speaking to Music

41. Singing Two-Note Motifs

42. Speaking More Complicated Cadence Motifs

43. Putting it All Together – Singing Motifs

44. Discovering Words through Emotion

45. Sound Symbols

46. Singing Sound Symbols

47. Internal Rhyme Story

48. Internal Rhyme Story in Rhythm

49. Internal Rhyme Story in Verse Form

Appendix B

Musical Tracks

1. Vocal Warm-up

2. Emotional Music (Shivar)

3. Emotional Music (Rosen)

4. Emotional Music (Pollock)

5. Emotional Music (Samuel)

6. Emotional Music (Koshi)

7. Sung Melody Samples (Walker)

8. Eight Beats of Music Loop (Gilbane)

9. Ear Training

10. Verse Melody Example

11. OneVerse (Anderson)

12. One Verse (Stern)

13. One Verse (Gilbane)

14. One Verse (Stern)

15. One Verse (Koshi)

16. Irish Drinking Song (Gilbane)

17. Word Melody Example (Walker)

18. Two Full Verses of music (Shivar)

19. Two Full Verses of music (Spitznagel)

20. Two Full Verses of music (Rosen)

21. Two Full Verses of music (Kaufman)

22. Two Full Verses of music(Descoteaux)

23. Hoedown (Samuel)

24. Blues (Pollock)

25. Full Tagline Song (Pollock)

26. Full Tagline Song (Ellis)

27. Full Tagline Song (Anderson)

28. Full Tagline Song (Bouthiette)

29. Full Tagline Song (Kaufman)

30. Two Choruses (Goetschel)

31. Two Choruses (Ellis)

32. Two Choruses (Anderson)

33. Two Choruses (Descoteaux)

34. Two Choruses (Koshi)

35. Full Verse Chorus Song (Anderson)

36. Full Verse Chorus Song (Spitznagel)

37. Full Verse Chorus Song (Bouthiette)

38. Full Verse Chorus Song (Webb)

39. Full Verse Chorus Song (Ellis)

40. Full Verse Chorus Bridge Song (Doo-Wop) (Gilbane)

41. Sondheim Verse (Shivar)

42. Sondheim Verse (Descoteaux)

43. Sondheim Verse (Shivar)

44. Sondheim Verse (Goetschel)

45. Sondheim Double Verse (Webb)

46. Sondheim Double Verse (Descoteaux)

47. Sondheim Tagline (Spitznagel)

48. Sondheim Full Song (Shivar)

49. Sondheim Full Song (Descoteaux)

50. Beethoven's Fifth (Skidmore College Orchestra)

51. Easy Harmony - Hearing Notes in Chords (Walker)

52. More Advanced Harmony (Walker)

53. "Song of the Angels" (Stern)

54. "Stars and Stripes Forever" Excerpt (Sousa, played by the US Marine Corps Band)

Appendix C

List of Games

101
Ballet
Modern Dance
Performance Art
Emotional Symphony
Dr. Know it all Song
Da Doo Ron Ron
Doo Wah Diddy
Make Up Your Own Nonsense Phrase Line Song
Irish Drinking Song
Generic Line Musical Improv Games

201
Hoedown
The Blues
Lounge Singer
Bartender

301
Creating your own musical games:
Short-Form Musical Games for the Whole Troupe
    (examples: Doo-Wop, Blues)

Appendix D

Topics

1. School

2. Politics

3. Vacation

4. Pets

5. Chocolate

6. Taxes

7. Driving

8. Work

9. Dogs

10. Cats

11. Parents

12. Restaurants

13. Marriage

14. Science

15. Sports

16. Sickness

17. Transportation

18. Sex

19. Camping

20. Religion

21. Clothes

22. Dentistry

23. Pirates

24. Energy

25. Agriculture

26. Airplanes

27. Banks

28. Movies

29. The Circus

30. Fantasy

31. Video Games

32. Witches

33. Natural Disasters

34. Crime/Justice

35. Junk Food

36. War

37. Celebrities

38. Evolution

39. Holidays

40. Aliens

Appendix E

Song Titles

If you need some titles to sing practice songs, just pick a number from 1 – 220. Some of these titles come from musical improv classes I've taught, where I've remembered to collect the extra song titles the participants wrote out...

1. My Aching *Feet*

2. By the *Fountain*

3. Graying *Beard*

4. The *Man* Lightly Snoring Beside Me

5. Picnic by the *Lake*

6. Empty *Beach*

7. Let's Go to the *Movies*

8. I Can *Breathe* Again

9. Where Do You Get the *Balls*

10. Big Ol' *Feet*

11. Kiss My *Grits*

12. I *Love* Your Love

13. She Had Obama *Ears*

14. Too Much *Wax* in Your Ears

15. Soft as a *Baby's Bottom*

16. Get off My *Back*

17. *Ex-Lovers* on a Plane

18. *Drive* the Car

19. *Sheriff's* Come to Town

20. Strangle Me *Softly*

21. Why 3.14?

22. Dharma's Nuisance

23. Let's Be Honest

24. Crossing the Line

25. I've Grown Allergic to your Face

26. Working for Hours, Sleeping for Longer

27. Scarred by Doves

28. After All, Love Tickles

29. Pick My Brain

30. In Bed Next to You

31. Wake Up

32. Childhood Friend

33. Elaborate Please

34. GiddyApp!

35. Red Stain

36. Dog Whisperer

37. Formal Night on the Cruise

38. Squeaky Hinge

39. Saucy Animals

40. Chippendale's Drunk

41. Partners for Life

42. Oogle-eyed Dog

43. Zing!

44. Diamond Door Knob

45. I Just Wanna Sleep

46. I Kin Read My Kindle

47. Sudoku Fog

48. Mickey Mouse

49. Central Air

50. Facebook Friends

51. French Lick

52. Eagle Nest

53. Eek!

54. Blue Green Love

55. Lazy Days

56. My Grandma was Your Grandpa

57. Diggity Dang

58. Turn Your Head and Cough

59. Cool Shadows

60. Letting Go

61. Spread Eagle

62. Par Five

63. Summer Haze

64. I Gotta Itch

65. Brothers

66. Snark Attack

67. The Earlobe Nibbler

68. Ankle Deep

69. Looking at the Moon

70. Here She Comes

71. Little Bird

72. Meh.

73. Rest Your Weary X

74. Fuzzy Cheek

75. Fuzzy Balls

76. Tonsillitis

77. Cute Q-tip

78. My Bowtie's too Tight

79. Cynicism

80. Snuggle Up

81. Curious Kumquat

82. Purring Perfection

83. Baby Boy

84. Momma's Muscled Men

85. Are You Comfy There

86. Singing a Single in Singapore

87. Just a Jew

88. Littered with Alliterations

89. Literally Alliterative

90. I'm Going Home to Mother

91. Pack My Bags

92. Toe Jam Blues

93. Smarmy Shuffle

94. In Irons

95. Fiberglass and Wool

96. Cats and Dogs

97. Critters and Doors

98. Roll Me Home

99. Avast Ye Mateys

100. Turn Out the Lights

101. Ching Ching

102. Cold Snap

103. It only Takes Five Minutes

104. We're Out of Jimmy Dean

105. Where Are You

106. You're Not Rolling Yet

107. Passed Out On the Bed

108. Abandoned Mine

109. The Deserted Beach

110. Ominous Lady

111. You're Standing Between Me and My Clothes

112. Sideways Glance

113. Criminal Intent

114. Wife Killer
115. TV Celebrity
116. I Have a Problem with That
117. On the Same Page
118. Little Man Behind the Curtain
119. Something Very Personal
120. Do You Have to Be Here
121. People Like You
122. A Stupid Joke
123. Up to No Good
124. The Birthday Suit
125. The Crime Scene
126. Falsely Accused
127. Someone You'll Never Find
128. Crushed Flower
129. Probable Cause
130. Desperate Accusations
131. An Airtight Case
132. My Milk has Soured
133. Something Like a Rose
134. Father and Son
135. He's Not My Type
136. Don't Trust Anyone in a Suit
137. Do You Mind
138. On the Wrong Track

139. (I'm Not Making it Official but) I Want You to Withdraw

140. I'm Not Grieving, Are You

141. You Made Your Point

142. You've the Best I've Got

143. Married for the Fourth Time

144. Why the Sudden Loss of Control

145. The Guy's a Charmer

146. Tuesdays at Ten

147. I was a Flirt

148. How I Got the Job

149. Up to Date

150. Interrogation One

151. You Have a Generic Face

152. You'd Never....You Know

153. Keep This Quiet

154. Swizzle Stick

155. KFC Night Out

156. Look, But Don't Play

157. Triple Threat

158. Double Blessed

159. Movin' and Groovin' to the Tune

160. Stand in Line

161. It Worked Out Well

162. Buzz Me In

163.Good Cop, Bad Cop

164.Wandering Aimlessly

165.My Brand

166.I Said No

167.A Poisoned Pill

168.Out and Out Dumb

169.Worse, Worse, Worse

170.I Know and I Am

171.Never the Sandbox

172.Don't Make Me Beg

173.Don't Laugh at Me

174.Was Revenge Sweet

175.The Way it Works

176.A Silver Cummerbund

177.I'm a Good Friend

178.Patch Things Up

179.Glad I'm Not Rich

180.It's Not an Act

181.In a Pitiful Kind of Way

182.The Broken Glass Table

183.Lost Puppy

184.Dead Eyes

185.To Fight or Flee

186.Down at the Station

187.That's Real Hate

188. Sweet Space

189. Problem Mom

190. Crash On the Couch

191. You Don't Love Him, You Only Need Him

192. You Cut Me Out

193. Glad I Went to Public School

194. You Serve My Need

195. Possession

196. Drop My Heart

197. What a Damn Shame

198. How About Last Night

199. How Many Witnesses Do You Need

200. Traitor in Our Midst

201. Always Good to Me

202. When the Time Came

203. Sittin' in a Cabana

204. The Perfect Cruise

205. A Bad Year for Boeing

206. Location Location Location

207. Reefer Sadness

208. Amateur to Ace

209. Poser to Pro

210. I Don't Give a Damn

211. He Don't Roll That Way

212. Winning

Appendix F

Song Styles

As an improviser, you should be aware of and able to perform in various styles. As a musical improviser, whether the audience dictates the musical style for you or it's left open, you should be knowledgeable in most of the following styles. (You don't want all your songs to sound the same, so switching up styles is important!)

Typical Styles (ones often shouted out by audiences)

Bebop

Blues

Calypso

Christian Rock

Classical

Classic Rock

Country & Western

Disco

Doo-wop

Folk

Funk

Gospel

Gregorian Chant

Heavy Metal

Jazz

Opera

Polka

Pop

Punk

R&B/Soul

Rap/Hip-Hop

Reggae

Ska

Techno

More Obscure Styles

Alternative Rock

Baroque

Black Metal

Boys Band

Brit pop

Chanson

Christmas songs

Darkwave

Death Metal

Europop

Glam

Grunge

Industrial

New wave

Nu metal

Psychedelic Rock

Rockabilly

Shoegaze

Techno

Trance

Triphop

Styles of Composers

* Rodgers & Hart (witty, slightly sexual, urbane... "Bewitched, Bothered and Bewildered" "Lady is a Tramp")

* Rodgers & Hammerstein (more innocent, tends to be upbeat... South Pacific, Sound of Music, Okalahoma, King & I)

* Porter (high class, socialite stuff... "In the Still of the Night")

* Sondheim (wordy, lists, alliterations, rhymes...*Company, Into the Woods, Sweeny Todd*)

Index

Trios
194,196
"Triumph"
169
Trochaic
144

V

Variety
198-202
Verses
17-19,42,50-51,54,59-60,63,66-
71,73-78,83-90,93-107,110,118-
119,121-124,132,134,142-143,
148,159,166,172,186,194-197
Verse Chorus Songs
107119,124,129,131,194,198,
202
Verse Songs
87-96,101,196

W

Waits, Tom
174
Waltz Time
18
Warm-up
4-6,27-28,133
Webb, Jimmy
93
Webb, Lisa
216
Whiting
104

Whose Line is it, Anyway?
73,78,88
Wu Wei
7,127

Z

Zenprov
20,70

Made in the USA
Charleston, SC
11 August 2012